OpenOffice 3.4
Volume I: Writer

quantum scientific publishing

OpenOffice 3.4
Volume I: Writer

CHRISTOPHER N. CAIN

RILEY W. WALKER

quantum scientific publishing

OpenOffice 3.4
Volume I: Writer

ISBN-13: 978-1480224322
ISBN-10: 1480224324

Published by quantum scientific publishing

Pittsburgh, PA | Copyright © 2012

All rights reserved. Permission in writing must be obtained from the publisher before any part of this work may be reproduced or transmitted in any form, including photocopying and recording.

OpenOffice and the OpenOffice logo are trademarks or registered trademarks of The Apache Software Foundation and/or its affiliates.

Cover design by Scott Sheariss

Table of Contents

Unit One

Section 1.1 – Introduction to OpenOffice Writer   2

Section 1.2 – Tips and the Help Dialog Box   5

Section 1.3 – Creating a Writer Document   9

Section 1.4 – Saving a Writer Document   13

Section 1.5 – Closing a Writer Document   17

Section 1.6 – Printing a Writer Document   20

Section 1.7 – Saving a File in a Different Format   26

Section 1.8 – Opening an Existing Document   29

Section 1.9 – Changing the Document Margins and Orientation   32

Section 1.10 – Different Views Available in Writer   38

Section 1.11 – Viewing the Navigator in Writer   40

Section 1.12 – Creating Envelopes and Labels   45

Section 1.13 – Getting Started with Mail Merge   51

Section 1.14 – Creating a Salutation in Mail Merge   57

Section 1.15 – Editing the Mail Merge   61

Unit Two

Section 2.1 – Editing a Writer Document   68

Section 2.2 – Checking Spelling and Grammar   72

Section 2.3 – Inserting Page Numbers   78

Section 2.4 – Inserting the Date and Time   82

Section 2.5 – The Thesaurus, Dictionary, and Word Count   89

Section 2.6 – Using the Translator's Tools   97

Section 2.7 – Adding a Hyperlink to the Document   101

Section 2.8 – Creating an Outline   107

Section 2.9 – Finding and Replacing Text   112

Section 2.10 – Using AutoCorrect   117

Section 2.11 – Creating a Table   121

Section 2.12 – Using AutoText   125

Section 2.13 – Formatting Tables   129

Section 2.14 – Working with Table Data   134

Section 2.15 – Using Columns to Present Text   138

Unit Three

Section 3.1 – Changing Font, Color, and Size   144

Section 3.2 – Using the Fontwork Gallery and ClipArt   149

Section 3.3 – Adding Headers and Footers to a Document   155

Section 3.4 – Adding Footnotes and Endnotes to a Document   159

Section 3.5 – Creating Custom Tab Stops   162

Section 3.6 – Indenting Text in a Document   165

Section 3.7 – Changing the Horizontal Alignment   169

Section 3.8 – Inserting a Manual Page Break   173

Section 3.9 – Adjusting Line Spacing in a Document   176

Section 3.10 – Using the Borders and Shading Tool   180

Section 3.11 – Using the Bullets and Numbering Tool   186

Section 3.12 – Sorting a List   188

Section 3.13 – Adding Symbols and Special Characters to a Document   191

Section 3.14 – Using Styles in a Document   194

Section 3.15 – Creating New Styles in Writer   199

Appendix

OpenOffice Volume I: Writer Answer Key   208

Unit One

Section 1.1 – Introduction to OpenOffice Writer   2

Section 1.2 – Tips and the Help Dialog Box   5

Section 1.3 – Creating a Writer Document   9

Section 1.4 – Saving a Writer Document   13

Section 1.5 – Closing a Writer Document   17

Section 1.6 – Printing a Writer Document   20

Section 1.7 – Saving a File in a Different Format   26

Section 1.8 – Opening an Existing Document   29

Section 1.9 – Changing the Document Margins and Orientation   32

Section 1.10 – Different Views Available in Writer   38

Section 1.11 – Viewing the Navigator in Writer   40

Section 1.12 – Creating Envelopes and Labels   45

Section 1.13 – Getting Started with Mail Merge   51

Section 1.14 – Creating a Salutation in Mail Merge   57

Section 1.15 – Editing the Mail Merge   61

Section 1.1 – Introduction to OpenOffice Writer

Section Objective:

- Learn how to get started with OpenOffice Writer by identifying the features on the application window.

Introduction

Welcome to OpenOffice Writer. Writer is a free and powerful word processing tool, and is just one of six applications found within the Apache OpenOffice Suite 3.4. If not already installed, download the latest version of the Apache OpenOffice Suite from the www.openoffice.org website. When the page loads, click "I want to download OpenOffice" to be directed to the download page. Follow the instructions to complete the download.

This book begins by introducing the basic features and layout of Writer, and then progresses to more complex functions and operations. At the end of each section, there are questions which test readers' understanding of the application. Use these questions, as well as the steps provided in this book, to learn many different tasks which can be accomplished in OpenOffice Writer.

Features in OpenOffice Writer

There are a series of drop-down menus and toolbars in OpenOffice Writer. All of the needed tools are located in these features and can be accessed by clicking on the Menu Bar options and selecting the desired tool from the drop-down menus.

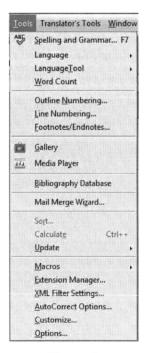

Figure 1

The tools for each menu are divided into groups (such as the Graphics, Links, and Text tools in Writer's Insert menu). Some tools located on the drop-down menus are context-sensitive, meaning they only display when a particular feature is being used. For example, when a table is inserted into a document, additional table tools and options will be available in the Table menu.

Dialog Boxes

Many of the tools in Writer have dialog boxes. These dialog boxes provide additional options. For example, when inserting a table using the Table menu, Writer will display a dialog box which provides advanced features and settings for the inserted table.

Figure 2

Shortcut Icons

Writer has shortcut icons for the most commonly used tools. These shortcuts are located on the Toolbar. The name of the tool will appear when the cursor is positioned over the shortcut, and the tool can be used by clicking on the shortcut. For example, clicking on the Open toolbar icon will cause the Open dialog box to appear.

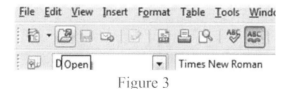

Figure 3

Growth & Assessment

1. Where would a user find all of the needed tools in Writer?

2. Steve is making a table in Writer to keep track of his monthly expenses. Once he has made the table, where would he find additional table tools and options?

3. Which feature allows users to easily access the most commonly used tools in Writer?

Section 1.2 – Tips and the Help Dialog Box

Section Objectives:

- Learn how to get help with OpenOffice Writer using Tips.

- Learn how to get help with OpenOffice Writer using the Help Dialog Box.

Tips

Writer has features that help the user identify tools and perform certain tasks. **Tips** is a feature that displays the name of the tool when the cursor is positioned over its shortcut on the Toolbar. This feature is helpful when trying to quickly identify a shortcut. Tips also displays other useful information in the document. For example, when scrolling through a document, Tips displays the current page number.

What's This?

What's This? is another feature in Writer that will display extended tips about the buttons available on the various toolbars. What's This? is also helpful when trying to understand the functionality of a command or the different uses of a button.

Accessing What's This?

The **What's This?** feature can be accessed by opening the Help menu and selecting What's This?. Once the feature is selected, the button's description will appear when the cursor is positioned over it. For example, if the What's This? feature is selected, and the cursor is positioned over the Spell Check button on the formatting toolbar, the extended tips will be displayed **(Figure 1)**.

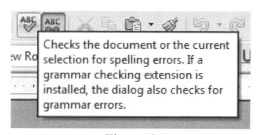

Figure 1

If a user would like to enable extended tips so that they are always displayed, this can be done by opening the Tools menu, selecting Options, choosing General (on the left, under OpenOffice.org), and enabling the "tips" and "extended tips" checkboxes **(Figure 2)**. By enabling these features, users are able to identify the name of a button and its functionality without opening the Help menus.

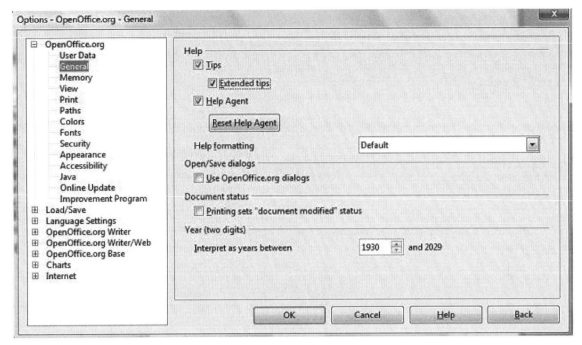

Figure 2

Help Dialog Box

In situations where the What's This? feature is enabled, but more information is needed, the information can be found in the Help Dialog Box. Accessing the Help Dialog Box is done by clicking the Help button, which is the small question mark, located in the upper right-hand corner of the Menu Bar **(Figure 3)**.

Figure 3

Here are some steps to follow when using the Help Dialog Box:

In this example, the user is attempting to save a document in Writer.

Step 1: Click the **Find** tab at the top of the Help Dialog Box, and in the Search textbox, type *saving a document.*

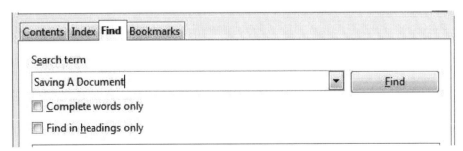

Figure 4

Step 2: Click **Find**, and the search results will appear in the Help Dialog Box.

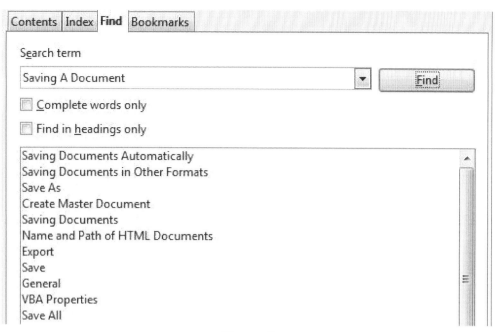

Figure 5

Step 3: Select **Save As** from the search results displayed. Once selected, a description of how to perform a Save As function will appear on the screen.

Figure 6

Step 4: When the needed information has been obtained, close the Help Dialog Box.

Growth & Assessment

1. What feature in OpenOffice Writer helps the user identify tools and perform tasks?

2. How do users access the What's This? feature?

3. If the What's This? feature is enabled and more information is needed, more information can be found by using the Help Dialog Box.

    a. TRUE

    b. FALSE

4. When using the Help Dialog Box to learn how to save a document, what is the first step?

Section 1.3 – Creating a Writer Document

Section Objective:

- Learn how to create a document in OpenOffice Writer.

Creating a Blank Document

Writer, by default, creates a new blank document when the program is opened. A new document can also be created by going through the Menu Bar; the steps are provided below.

Steps for Creating a New Blank Document Using the Menu Bar:

Step 1: Click **File**, which is located on the Menu Bar.

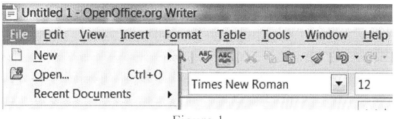

Figure 1

Step 2: Click **New**, and the New Document dialog box will appear.

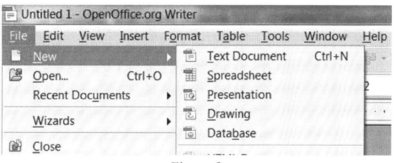

Figure 2

Step 3: Select the **Text Document** option.

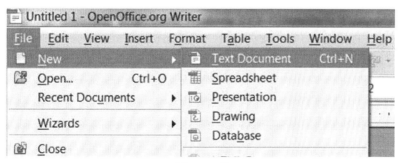

Figure 3

Creating a Template Document

Writer provides multiple templates for the user. Templates are documents with a pre-designed format which can be used for many types of documents. Writer has templates for letters, memos, resumes and other common types of documentation. By using these templates, a user can save time and add a professional look to a document with little effort. The templates can be downloaded for free, and the steps are outlined below.

Step 1: Visit the following link: *http://extensions.services.openoffice.org/node/950*.

Figure 4

Step 2: Scroll down and click on the **Get It!** button to be directed to the **Download** page.

Figure 5

Step 3: Click on the manual download link to begin the download.

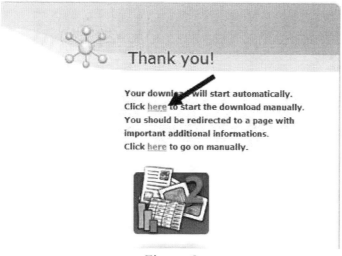

Figure 6

Step 4: When prompted, click on the **Open** button on the File Download window.

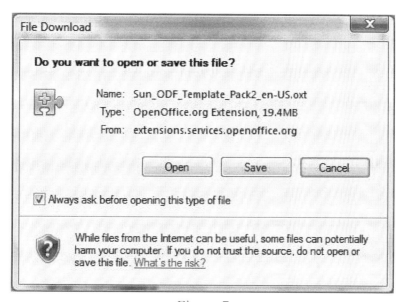

Figure 7

Step 5: Click **OK** to install the **Professional Template Pack II – English** and then click **Accept,** to accept the license agreement.

Figure 8

Step 6: The Extension Manager window will appear showing that the Template Pack has been added to Writer. Click **Close** and begin using the new templates.

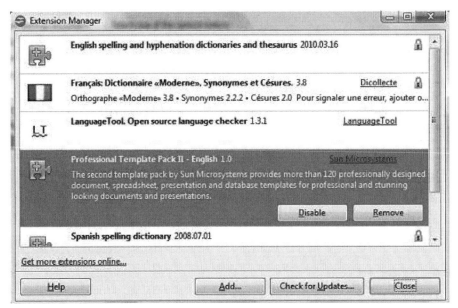

Figure 9

Growth & Assessment

1. When opening Writer, a new document will be created.

    a. TRUE

    b. FALSE

2. What is the third step in creating a blank document using the Menu Bar in Writer?

3. What are some of types of templates Writer has to offer? Give two examples.

Section 1.4 – Saving a Writer Document

Section Objective

- Learn how to save a document in OpenOffice.org Writer.

Saving a Document in Writer

In Writer, there are two options for saving documents. The user can either save a document manually, or set up Writer to automatically save documents. In both cases, Writer will overwrite the last saved state of the document. This means that if the document was saved previously, the new state of the document (the document that is currently being saved), will take its place.

Steps to save a file manually:

Step 1: Click **File** on the Menu Bar.

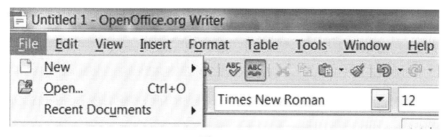

Figure 1

Step 2: Select **Save As**.

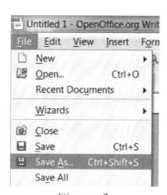

Figure 2

Step 3: The Save As dialog box will appear. When this happens, enter a file name and select the file type. If the document was previously saved, the new file, and file name, will take its place.

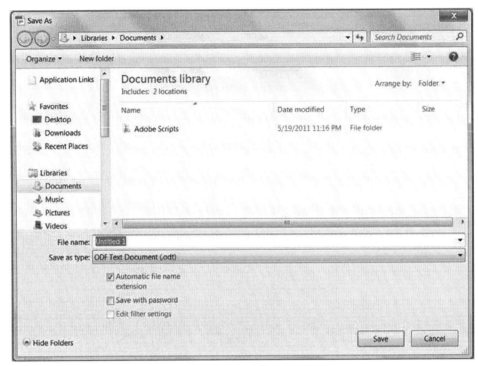

Figure 3

After the user has saved a document, and further alteration of the file has taken place, the user can click **File > Save** to quickly save the most recent version of the document.

Steps to set up automatic saving:

Step 1: Click **Tools,** which is located on the Menu Bar.

Figure 4

Step 2: Select **Options,** which is located at the bottom of the Tools drop-down menu.

Figure 5

Step 3: On the left side of the **Options** dialog box, under **Load/Save,** select **General.** Then, on the right side of the Options dialog box, click the checkbox next to **Save AutoRecovery information every.**

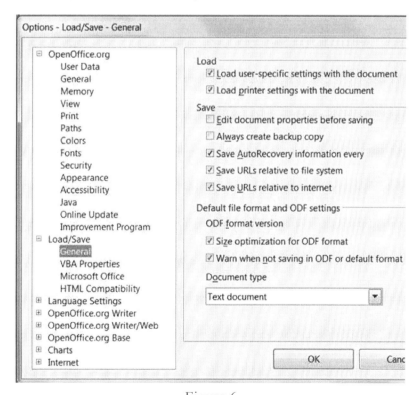

Figure 6

Step 4: Here the user is asked to select a desired time interval for Writer to automatically save the document. Click on the up or down arrows to select the desired time interval.

Growth & Assessment

1. How many options does Writer offer when saving files?

2. When saving a document, Writer will overwrite the last saved state of the document.

    a. TRUE

    b. FALSE

3. When manually saving a document in Writer, what must the user manually enter into the Save As dialog box?

Section 1.5 – Closing a Writer Document

Section Objective:

- Learn how to close a document in Writer.

Closing a Document in Writer

OpenOffice Writer gives the user two options when closing a document. One option is to close the document while keeping Writer open. This operation allows the user to easily access other options and open a new document. The other option is to close the document and exit out of the application (Writer) completely. Writer offers these two options so users can save time when opening and closing multiple documents.

Both closing options are outlined in the steps below:

Steps for closing a document while keeping Writer open:

Step 1: Open a previously created OpenOffice Writer document and make a change to the document.

Figure 1

Step 2: Click **File** on the Menu Bar. Once in the File drop-down menu, click **Close**. Since the document has new changes that have not yet been saved, a prompt will appear.

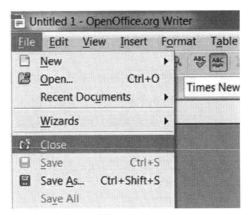

Figure 2

Step 3: Click **Save**, to save all recent changes to the document. After clicking Save, the document will close but the application (Writer) will remain open.

Figure 3

Closing a document and exiting the application:

Once a user has finished using the application (Writer), the application can be closed by clicking the **Close** button in the upper right-hand corner of the Writer window **(Figure 4)**. The application can also be closed by clicking **File** on the Menu Bar, and then selecting **Exit** from the File drop-down menu **(Figure 5)**.

Figure 4

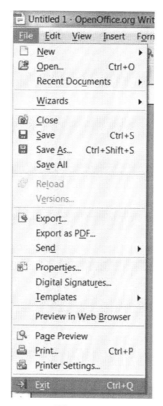

Figure 5

Growth & Assessment

1. In OpenOffice Writer, what are the two options for closing a document?

2. Selecting the Minimize button (Figure 6) in the upper right-hand corner of the Writer window will close the document and exit the application.

Figure 6

    a. TRUE

    b. FALSE

3. If a user wants to close a document in Writer and keep the application open, where is the Close button located?

Section 1.6 – Printing a Writer Document

Section Objectives:

- Learn how to print a document.

- Learn how to print specific pages.

- Learn how to print a closed document.

Printing a Document in Writer

Printing a document in Writer can be done several ways. One way is by going through the Print option in the File drop-down menu. Another way to print a document is by going through the Page Preview screen. The Page Preview screen allows the user to see what the document will look like when printed and can be useful in many situations. Both ways however, will allow the user to print a document, and the steps for these options are outlined below.

The third way to print, which is very useful and saves the user time, is by using the keyboard shortcut. The keyboard shortcut for printing is executed by pressing and holding the **CTRL** key and then pressing the **P** key, or simply **CTRL + P.** This shortcut will bring the user directly to the Print dialog box.

Steps to Printing a Document Using the Print Option in the File Menu:

Step 1: Click **File** on the Menu Bar.

Step 2: Select **Print** from the File drop-down menu. Once Print has been selected, the Print dialog box will appear.

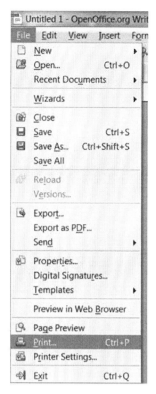

Figure 1

Step 3: Here, the user has many printing options. The user can select which printer to use, which pages to print, how many copies to print, the order in which the pages print, and additional printing options. Once the printing details have been selected, click **Print.**

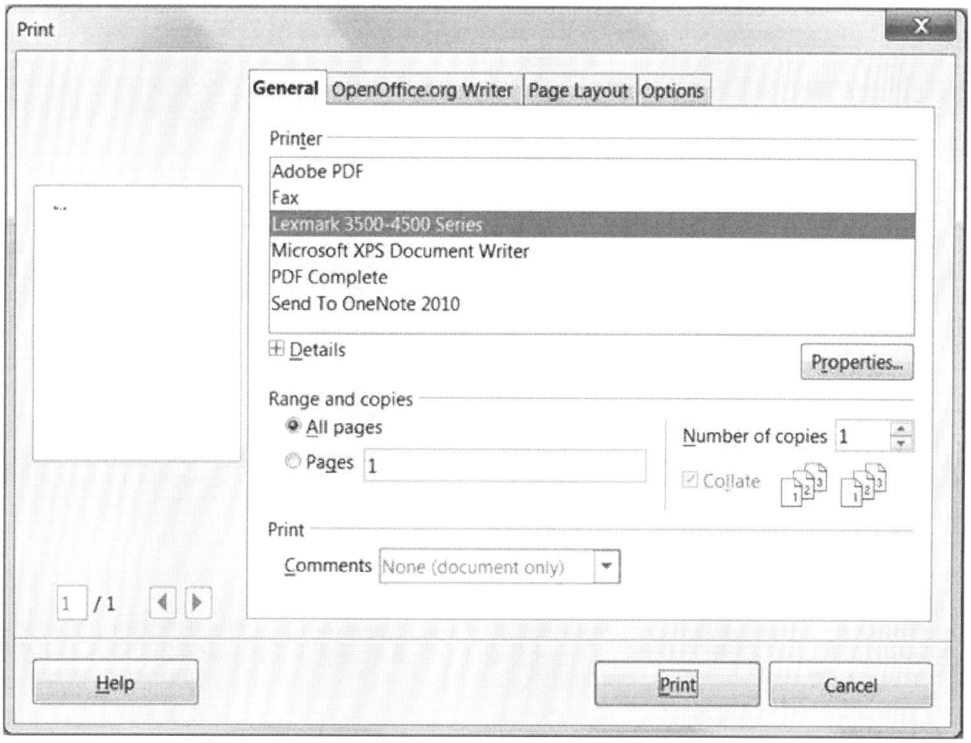

Figure 2

Steps to Printing a Document Using the Page Preview Screen:

Step 1: Click **File** on the Menu Bar.

Step 2: Within the File drop-down menu, select **Page Preview**. Once selected, the Page Preview screen will appear.

Figure 3

Step 3: The Page Preview screen will display a sample of what the document will look like when printed. If acceptable, click **Print** and the Print dialogue box will appear.

Step 4: Within the Print dialog box, the user has the option to select which pages to print, how many copies to print, the order in which the pages print, and additional printing options. Once the printing details have been selected, click **Print.**

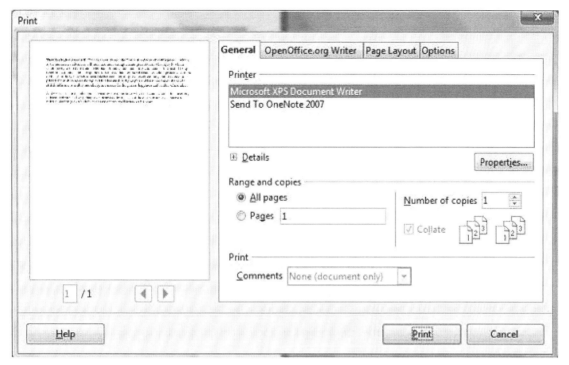

Figure 4

Printing Specific Pages of a Document

Writer provides many printing options. One particular option allows the user to identify which portions of the document to print. These printing options can be found in the Print dialog box which can be accessed by following the steps above. Some of the options found in the Print dialog box which correlate directly with the desired printed portions are, but not limited to, current page, selection, or non-contiguous pages. The steps for selecting these various printing options are outlined below.

Printing the Current Page

Step 1: Follow one of the steps above to access the Print dialog box.

Step 2: Once the Print dialog box has appeared, select **Pages** in the bottom left-hand corner.

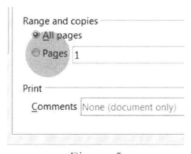

Figure 5

Step 3: Once Pages has been selected, enter the current page number in the textbox to the right and click Print.

23

Printing Non-Contiguous Pages

Step 1: Follow one of the steps above to access the Print dialog box.

Step 2: Once the Print dialog box has appeared, select **Pages** in the bottom left-hand corner.

Step 3: Type in the desired pages using dashes to specify page ranges and commas, or semicolons, to separate individual pages, or ranges. For example, if a document is 25 pages in length and pages one through four, page eight, and page twelve need to be printed, a user could select these pages by typing in the following: **1-4, 8, 12.**

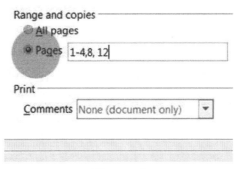

Figure 6

Printing a Closed Document in Writer

Writer allows users to quickly print documents without opening the documents. The following steps outline how this task can be done.

Step 1: Find the desired Writer document on the computer desktop.

Step 2: Right-click on the document and select **Print** from the drop-down menu.

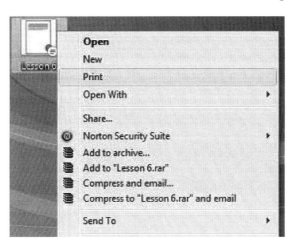

Figure 7

Step 3: The document will print to the default printer that has been specified.

Growth & Assessment

1. Name one way to print a document.

2. The keyboard shortcut for accessing the Print dialog box is CTRL+D.

    a. TRUE

    b. FALSE

3. What are some of the printing options in Writer? List two.

4. Explain how to use the keyboard shortcut when printing in Writer.

Section 1.7 – Saving a File in a Different Format

Section Objective:

- Learn how to save a file in a different format.

Different File Formats in Writer

The default file type in OpenOffice Writer is an OpenDocument Format, also known as an ODF file. The file extension for this file type is **.odt**. Though this is the default file type in Writer, the application provides multiple file extensions. A breakdown of some common file extensions available in Writer are outlined below.

Common OpenOffice Writer File Types and Extensions

.odt – ODF Text Document

> *Description:* ODF Text Document is the default file type in Writer. This file type will work in any version of OpenOffice Writer. This file type will work the best while learning how to use this application, though other file types may be used. ODF Text Document is a XML-based file format that is used for electronic documents such as presentations, spreadsheets and word processing documents.

.ott – ODF Text Document Template

> *Description:* ODF Text Document Template is the file type used for Writer's templates. The ".ot" stands for *OpenDocument template*, and the last letter represents the file type. In this case, the last 't' in '.ott' stands for *Text*, i.e., Writer.

.doc – Microsoft Word 97/2000/XP

> *Description:* Microsoft Word 97/2000/XP is the default file type for Microsoft Word 97-2003. This file extension, **.doc**, is one of the most commonly used file extensions in OpenOffice.

Saving a File in a Different Format

As mentioned above, there are multiple file extension options when saving a file in Writer; however, saving a file in a different format can be done with minimal effort. The following steps outline this process.

Step 1: Open a new Writer document and type something into the document.

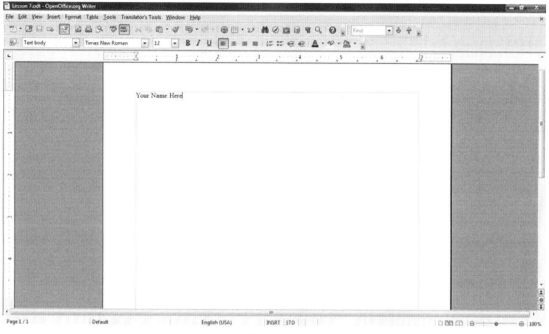

Figure 1

Step 2: Access to the **File** drop-down menu and select **Save As**. The Save As dialog box will appear.

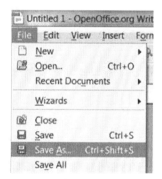

Figure 2

Step 3: Go to the **Save as Type** drop-down list. Here, the user is able to save the document in various formats which are all supported by OpenOffice Writer. Select the desired format, and click **Save**.

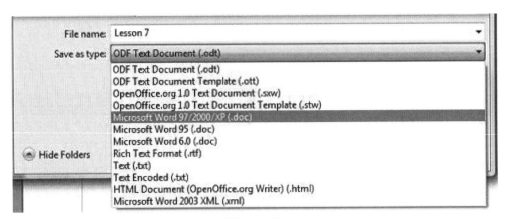

Figure 3

Growth & Assessment

1. OpenOffice Writer only offers one file extension when saving files.

    a. TRUE

    b. FALSE

2. Which file extension is used for an ODT Text Document?

3. Which file extension is used for an ODT Text Document Template?

4. What is the most commonly used file extension in Writer?

Section 1.8 – Opening an Existing Document

Section Objective:

- Learn how to open and view an existing document.

Open and View an Existing Document in Writer

In OpenOffice Writer, a user may not need to open a new document but instead, open an existing document to continue working. This section will cover two ways to open and view an existing document; accessing the document through the computer desktop, and accessing the document through the File drop-down menu.

Using the Desktop to Open and View an Existing Document

If a user wants to open an existing document from the computer desktop, the documents must be saved to the desktop. If the document has been saved to the desktop, opening and viewing the document can be done in two different ways. The first method of opening the document from the desktop is outlined in the steps below.

Step 1: Locate the document on the computer desktop. Depending on which operating system the computer has, the icon for a Writer document will look like the figure below.

Figure 1

Step 2: Double-click on the icon and the document will open in a Writer window.

Opening a document from the desktop can also be done by right-clicking on the document. The steps for this method of opening documents from the computer desktop are outlined in the steps below.

Step 1: Locate the document on the computer desktop. The icon for a Writer document is displayed in **Figure 1**.

Step 2: Right-click on the document; this will cause a pop-up menu to appear.

Step 3: Once the pop-up menu has appeared, click **Open**.

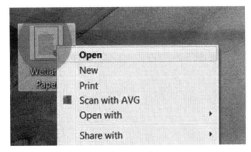

Figure 2

Writer also allows users to open existing documents from within the application. The steps for how this can be done are outlined below.

Step 1: Open OpenOffice Writer.

Step 2: Go to the Menu Bar and click **File**.

Step 3: Once in the File drop-down menu, select **Open**. Once Open has been selected, the Open dialog box will appear.

Step 4: On the left-hand side of the Open dialog box, there is a pane with links that navigate users to various folders; this is called the Navigation pane. Select the folder which contains the desired Writer document.

Figure 3

Step 5: Once in the folder, **right-click** the Writer document and click **Open**.

Opening and Viewing a Document as a Read Only

Writer also allows users to open a previously saved document as **Read Only**. A Read Only document allows the user to view the document; however, the user cannot make any alterations to the document. This feature is useful if the user is concerned about accidentally changing any of the content within the document. The following steps outline how this task is done.

Step 1: Open OppenOffice Writer.

Step 2: Go to the Menu Bar and click **File**.

Step 3: Once in the File drop-down menu, select **Open**. Once Open has been selected, the Open dialog box will appear.

Step 4: On the left-hand side of the Open dialog box there is a pane with links that navigate users to various folders; this is called the Navigation pane. Select the folder which contains the desired Writer document.

Step 5: Once in the folder, select the Writer document.

Step 6: Once the file has been selected, click the check box next to the text **Read-Only**. Once this has been done, the document name in the Title bar should have "**(Read -Only)**" beside it.

Figure 4

Growth & Assessment

1. If a user wants to open a document from the desktop, the document must first be saved onto the desktop.

    a. TRUE

    b. FALSE

2. Aside from accessing a saved document from the desktop, what is another option for opening a saved document?

3. Describe how to open a saved document from the desktop.

Section 1.9 – Changing the Document Margins and Orientation

Section Objectives:

- Learn how to change the margins of a document.
- Learn how to change the orientations of a document.

Changing the Margins in Writer

Margins are blank boarders that surround a document. Margins are usually are left blank, though text is sometimes found in the margins depending on the document. Some common text found within the margins are page numbers, headers and footers. Writer's default margins are set to 0.79 inches, for all four margins in the document. This tends to be wider than the default margins in Microsoft Word. If a user wishes to change the Margins in Writer there are several options; however, this section covers two of those options. The Margins can be changed by using the Page Rulers or by using the Format button located on the Menu Bar. Both ways are outlined in the steps below.

Changing Margins Using the Page Rulers

Step 1: Position the cursor over the line between the gray and white sections of the page ruler.

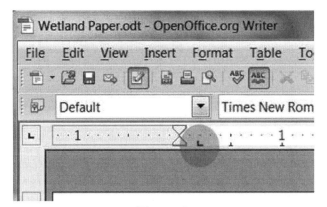

Figure 1

Step 2: Hold down the left mouse button and drag the line to adjust the margin for a particular side.

This feature is helpful when a user only wants to adjust one or two margins. If a user wants to adjust all four margins, using the Format button on the Menu Bar is much more efficient and the steps for this method are outlined below.

Changing Margins Using the Format Button

Step 1: Click **Format** on the Menu Bar to access the Format drop-down menu.

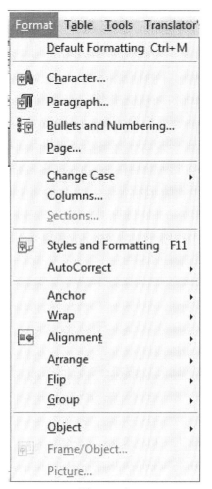

Figure 2

Step 2: Click **Page**, which will cause the **Page Style: Default** window to appear.

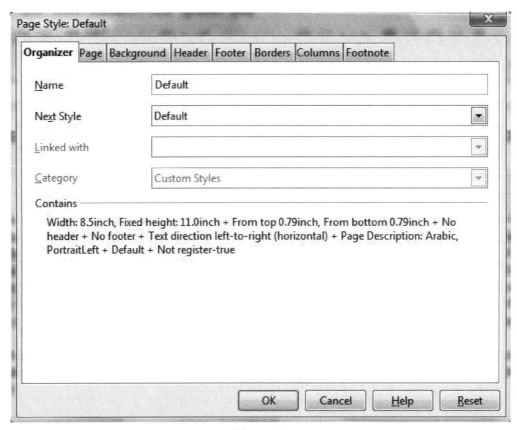

Figure 3

Step 3: Select the **Page** tab from the tabs located at the top of the window; this will cause the **Page Subscreen** to appear.

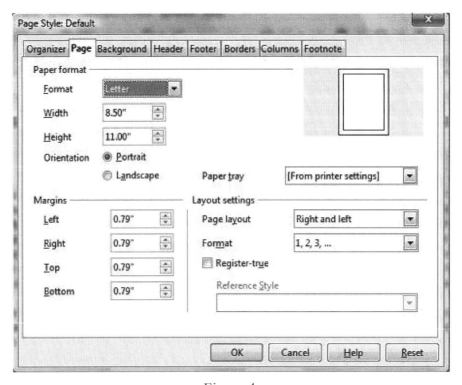

Figure 4

Step 4: In the bottom left-hand side of the window there will be four textboxes. Here, all four margins (top, bottom, left, and right), can be adjusted by typing in the desired width into the four textboxes.

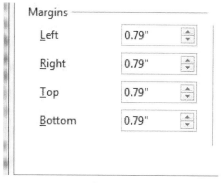

Figure 5

Changing the Orientations in Writer

Writer provides two different orientation options. The orientation options that are available are **Portrait** (vertical) and **Landscape** (horizontal). Writer allows users to change the orientation for the entire document, individual pages, and even individual paragraphs. The following steps outline how this task is done.

Step 1: Click **Format** on the Menu Bar to access the Format drop-down menu.

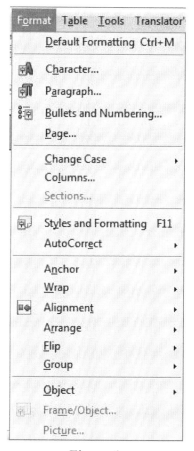

Figure 1

Step 2: Click **Page**, which will cause the **Page Style: Default** window to appear.

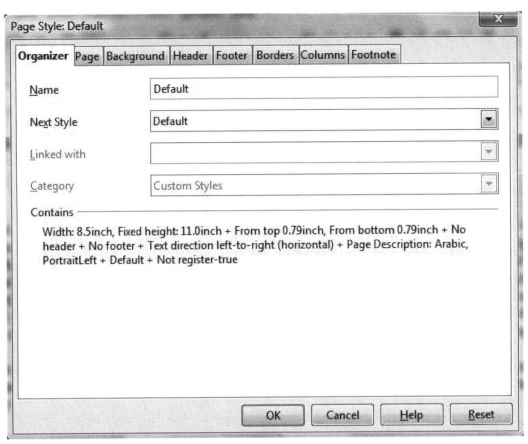

Figure 2

Step 3: Select the **Page** tab from the tabs located at the top of the window; this will cause the **Page Subscreen** to appear.

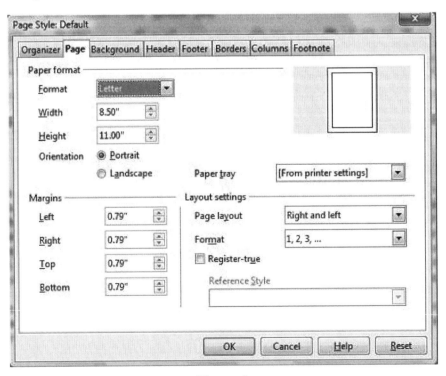

Figure 3

Step 4: There are radio buttons located in the top left-hand corner of the window. Select **Portrait** or **Landscape** depending on preference, and then click **OK**.

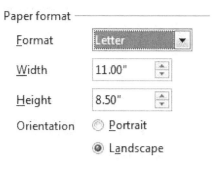

Figure 5

Writer also allows, as stated above, individual paragraphs and pages to have their own orientation. This can be done by selecting the desired text and following the steps above. Once the Page Subscreen appears, the user has the option of choosing the orientation for the selected text.

Growth & Assessment

1. What are two ways to change the Margins in Writer?

2. When adjusting Margins using the Page Rulers, where should the cursor be positioned?

3. What are the two orientation options available in Writer?

4. Margins can be changed through the Format button located on the Menu Bar.

    a. TRUE

    b. FALSE

Section 1.10 – Different Views Available in Writer

Section Objectives:

- Learn about the different views available in Writer.
- Learn how to change views in Writer.

Different Views Available in Writer

OpenOffice Writer provides three options for viewing a document. These views are provided to give the user alternative perspectives when working on a document. Below, the three views available in Writer are listed with a brief description.

Print Layout View – The Print Layout View is the default view in Writer. This view is designed to show how a document will look once it is printed. This view shows all of the original elements of the document, such as the headers, footers and page numbers.

Web Layout View – The Web Layout View shows how a document will look as a Web page.

Full Screen Reading View – The Full Screen Reading View is designed to make it easier to read a document. It shows the complete page on the screen, eliminating the need to scroll down the pages within a document.

Changing Views in Writer

Writer makes changing the view of a document very simple. The following three steps outline this process.

Step 1: Open Writer. Writer will automatically open in Print Layout View.

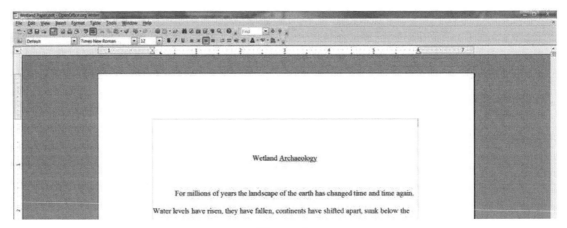

Figure 1

Step 2: Click **View** on the Menu Bar to access the View drop-down menu.

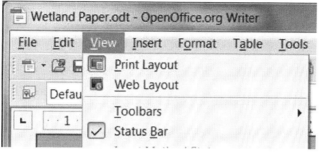

Figure 2

Step 3: Select the desired view.

Growth & Assessment

1. What are the three views available in Writer?

2. Web Layout View is the default view in Writer.

    a. TRUE

    b. FALSE

3. Full Screen Reading View allows the user to easily read the document without scrolling through the pages.

    a. TRUE

    b. FALSE

Section 1.11 – Viewing the Navigator in Writer

Section Objectives:

- Learn how to view the Navigator.
- Learn how to preview multiple pages.

Viewing the Navigator in Writer

The Navigator is a feature of OpenOffice Writer that allows users to quickly navigate through a document. This feature is helpful when writing research papers and other long documents. Navigator allows users to view the document as an outline and pinpoint which section of the paper they would like to go to without the hassle of scrolling through multiple pages. Locating and using the Navigator can be done by following the steps below.

Step 1: Open a previously saved document in Writer.

Step 2: Click **View** on the Menu Bar.

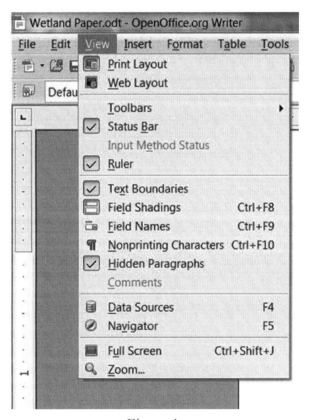

Figure 1

Step 3: In the View drop-down menu, select **Navigator;** this will cause the Navigator dialog box to appear.

Figure 2

Step 4: Click on the different headings listed in the Navigator to view different sections within the document.

Preview Multiple Pages in Writer

Writer allows for multiple pages to be viewed simultaneously (`at the same time), which is helpful when editing or proofreading multiple pages. This can be done by using the Zoom feature. The following steps will outline how to use Zoom.

Step 1: Click **View** on the Menu Bar to access the View drop-down menu.

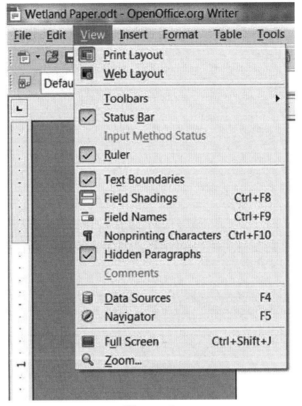

Figure 1

Step 2: Select **Zoom** from the View drop-down menu. This will cause the **Zoom & View Layout** window to appear on the screen.

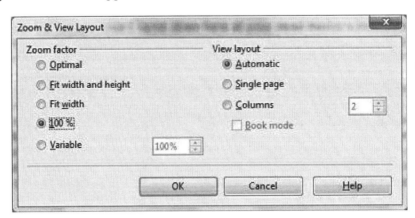

Figure 2

Step 3: On the Zoom & View Layout window, click the **Variable** radio button. Here, the user has the ability to choose how zoomed in, or zoomed out, the view of the document is by selecting the desired percentage.

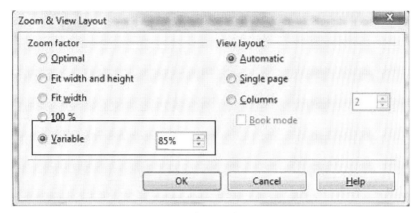

Figure 3

Step 4: Once a percentage has been identified, click **OK**.

Writer provides other ways of viewing multiple pages at once. The Layout buttons and Zoom scrollbar are features in Writer that allow the user to easily manipulate the Zoom and preview multiple pages simultaneously. These tools are located in the bottom right-hand corner of the application window. The following steps outline how this task is done.

Step 1: Click on the **View Pages Side by Side** icon located in the bottom right-hand corner of the application window. When the icon is clicked, the first two pages of the document will be displayed side by side.

Figure 1

Step 2: Use the Zoom scrollbar, found beside the Layout icons, to adjust the Zoom. Scroll to the left to lessen the percentage (zoom out) and scroll to the right to increase the percentage (zoom in). By scrolling the Zoom scrollbar to the left, more pages of the document will be displayed on the screen.

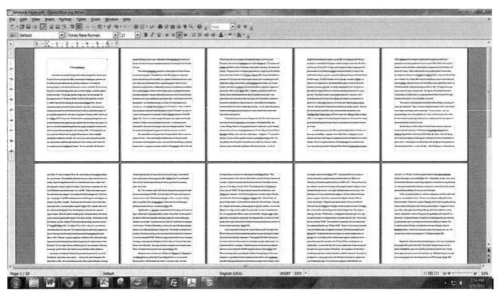

Figure 2

Growth & Assessment

1. Which features in Writer allow users to quickly search for sections of a document?

2. The View Pages Side by Side feature is located at the bottom left-hand corner of the application window.

    a. TRUE

    b. FALSE

3. What is the purpose of the Zoom feature?

Section 1.12 – Creating Envelopes and Labels

Section Objective:

- Learn how to create envelopes and labels.

Creating an Envelope in Writer

OpenOffice Writer has the capability to create a template that allows users to print an address directly on an envelope or label. This is useful when multiple letters, checks, or other common mailers need to be produced quickly and efficiently. The following steps outline how to create an envelope and label for a specific address.

Step 1: Open Writer and type, or open, the desired document.

Step 2: Click **Insert** on the Menu Bar.

Step 3: In the Insert drop-down menu, select **Envelope**. The Envelope dialog box will appear.

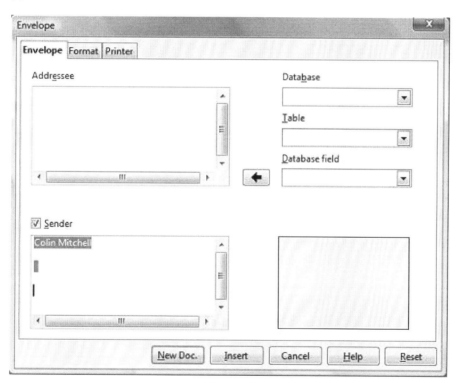

Figure 1

Step 4: Type the address of the person or business receiving the envelope, as well as the return address in the **Addressee** and **Sender** address fields.

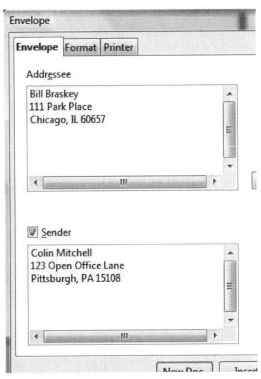

Figure 2

Step 5: After entering the information into the different address fields, Writer provides users with two options that are described below.

Option 1: In the Envelope dialog box, click **Insert**. This will place the recently created envelope beside the current document in the application window. This method is useful because it positions the envelope next to the document so if further editing needs to be completed, the user can add to the document as necessary.

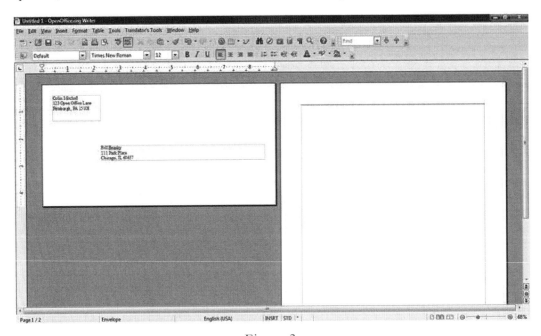

Figure 3

Option 2: In the Envelope dialog box, click **New Doc.** This will open a new application window with only the new envelope featured within it. This method is useful if the user wants to save the envelope separately to use at a later time.

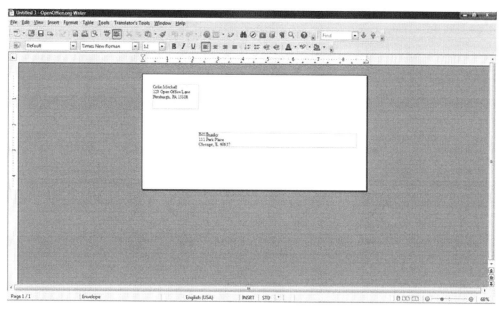

Figure 4

To modify the features of the Envelope, select the **Format** tab along the top of the Envelope dialog box. The Format window is divided into three sections:

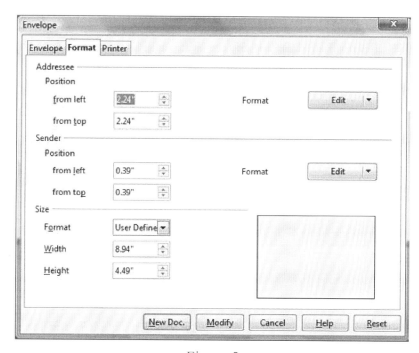

Figure 5

Addressee: Here, the user can change the address for the person or business that will be receiving the envelope.

Sender: Here, the user can change the envelope's return address.

Size: Here, the user can change the physical size of the envelope.

47

Writer provides a collection of pre-loaded envelope sizes which can be found in the **Size** drop-down menu. Writer also provides the option to change the size manually if the default sizes are not preferred.

Printing an Envelope in Writer

After creating an envelope in Writer, the application makes it easy for the user to print the envelope. The following steps outline how this process is done.

Step 1: Click on the **Print** tab located along the top of the Envelope dialog box.

Step 2: Select the envelope's orientation by clicking on one of the six different orientation options, as well as indicating whether the envelope should print from the top, or from the bottom.

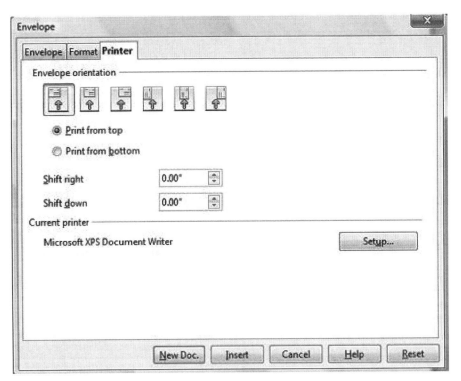

Figure 6

Step 3: Place a blank envelope into the printer, as indicated by the orientation image selected in Step 2, and click **Print**.

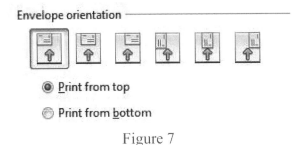

Figure 7

Creating Labels in Writer

Writer allows users to print an address on an individual label or print the same address on a full sheet of labels. This process is similar to the creation of an envelope. The following steps outline this process.

Step 1: Click **File** on the Menu Bar.

Step 2: Within the File drop-down menu, select **New** and then click **Labels**.

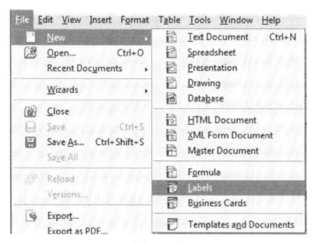

Figure 8

Step 3: The **Labels** dialog box will appear with the **Labels** tab selected by default.

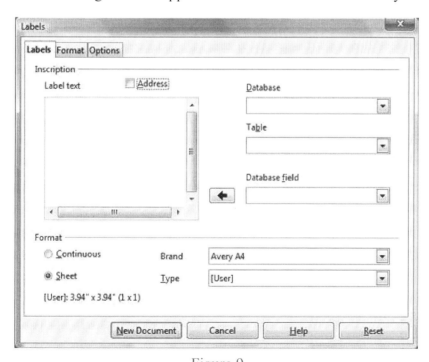

Figure 9

Step 4: Select the **Database**, **Table**, **Brand** and **Type** of Label desired. The Type of Label desired can be specified in the **Format** tap located along the top of the Label dialog box.

Step 5: Click **New Document**, which is located at the bottom of the Label dialog box. Once clicked, a page of labels will be created.

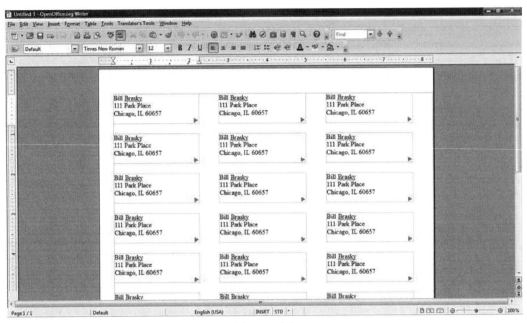

Figure 10

Note – To pint a single label, click the Options tab then select the Single label radio button.

Growth & Assessment

1. Writer cannot be used to create envelopes or labels.

    a. TRUE

    b. FALSE

2. Which tab, within the Envelope dialog box, should be selected when trying to modify the features of the Envelope?

3. How many sections make up the Format window of the Envelope dialog box? What are the different sections?

4. Which section in the Format window of the Envelope dialog box allows the user to change the return address?

Section 1.13 – Getting Started with Mail Merge

Section Objectives:

- Learn how begin the Mail Merge using the Mail Merge Wizard.

- Learn how to create a Mail Merge address book.

Creating a Mail Merge Address Book Using the Mail Merge Wizard

Mail Merge is a feature in OpenOffice Writer that is used for organizing multiple contacts. This feature allows users to create multiple documents with different Data Fields where contact information can be stored (Names, Addresses, etc…), all from a single template. Mail Merge is useful when one document needs to be mailed to multiple people or businesses.

Writer makes creating a Mail Merge easy through the **Mail Merge Wizard** feature. The Mail Merge Wizard gives step by step instruction explaining how to create a Mail Merge. The steps below outline how to access the Mail Merge Wizard.

Step 1: Open a new Writer document. From the **Tools** drop-down menu, select the **Mail Merge Wizard**.

Step 2: The Mail Merge Wizard dialog box will appear with the **Select Starting Document** screen.

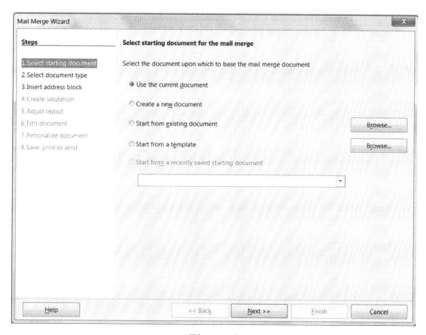

Figure 1

The Select Starting Document screen allows users to choose the base, or beginning document, that will be used as a template for all future documents used in Mail Merge. The options available include:

- Use the current document
- Create a new document
- Start from existing document
- Start from a template
- Start from a recently saved starting document

*For this example, choose **Create a New Document**, and click **Next**.

Step 3: Select the desired document type, either **Letter** or **E-mail message**. When a document type is selected, a brief description of that type of document will be described in the Mail Merge Wizard dialog box. After selecting the document type, click **Next**.

Note – For this example, choose **Letter**.

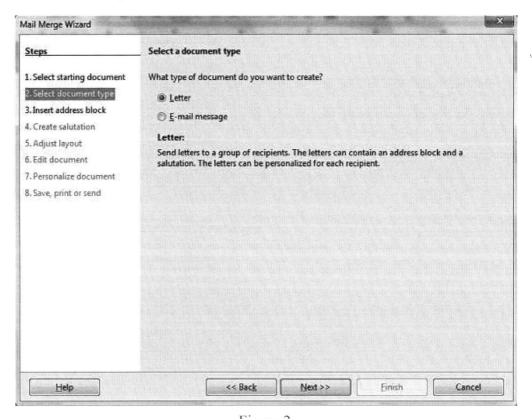

Figure 2

Step 4: In the **Insert address block** screen, click the **Select Address List** button at the top of the window. The Select Address List dialog box will open.

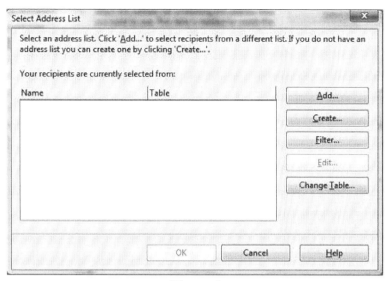

Figure 3

Step 5: Click **Create** to start a new address book. The New Address List window will appear containing all of the necessary fields to be completed.

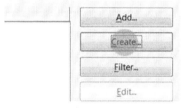

Figure 4

Step 6: Enter the Title, First Name, Last Name, Address, City, and Zip Code into the address book.

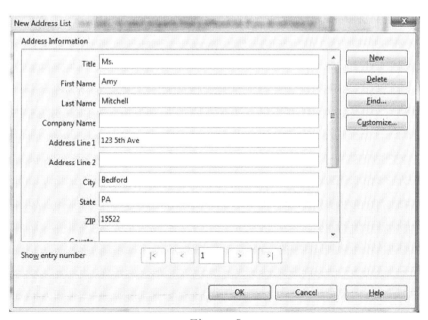

Figure 5

53

Step 7: Once finished with the first address, click **New** to enter the next name and address. Continue clicking **New** until all needed addresses have been entered and then click **OK**. This will direct the user to the **Save As** dialog box.

> **Note** – Writer allows users to look at the addresses entered by scrolling through the **Show Entry Number** list, located at the bottom of the New Address List window.

Figure 6

Step 8: Once directed to the Save As dialog box, enter a name for the recently created address book, and click **Save**. This will save the address book for future use.

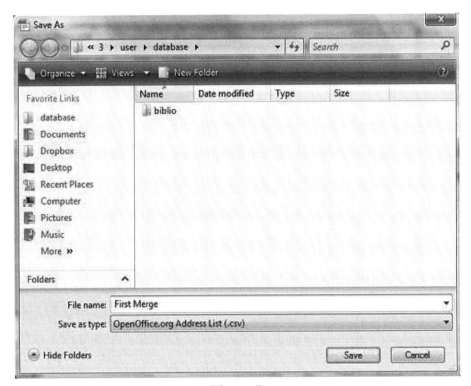

Figure 7

Step 9: After saving the address book, the Mail Merge Wizard directs the user back to the **Select Address List** window. Select the recently created address book and click **OK**. This will direct the user back to the **Insert address block** screen of the Mail Merge Wizard.

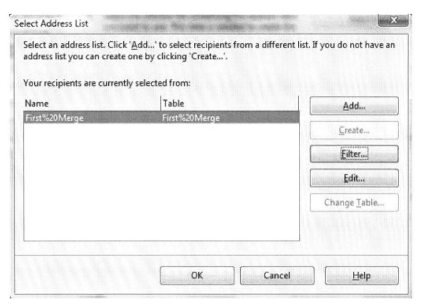

Figure 8

Step 10: If it is not already checked, click the checkbox beside **This Document Shall Contain an Address Block**.

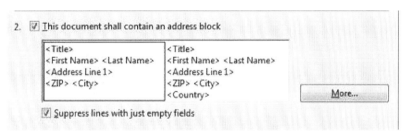

Figure 9

55

Step 11: In the **#3 Section** of the Insert Address Block screen, the Wizard allows the user to manually match the field names with the data that has been entered. Do this by clicking on the **Match Fields** button. This will cause the **Match Fields** dialog box to appear. Here, the Wizard allows the user to make any necessary changes. Once the necessary changes have been made, click **OK**.

Figure 10

Step 12: Check that the address data matches correctly with the entered information. Viewing the entered addresses can be done by scrolling through the **Insert address block** screen. After confirming that the addresses are correct, click **Next**. This is the final step for creating an address book using the **Mail Merge Wizard**.

Growth & Assessment

1. OpenOffice Writer uses Merge Mail to organize multiple contacts.

    a. TRUE

    b. FALSE

2. List three different options found within the Select Starting Document window.

3. After opening a new document under the Select Starting Document window, what two document types are provided?

4. What does the Match Fields option allow the user to do?

Section 1.14 – Creating a Salutation in Mail Merge

Section Objectives:

- Learn how to create a salutation in Mail Merge.

- Learn how to adjust the page layout in Mail Merge.

Creating a Salutation in Mail Merge

OpenOffice Writer offers a useful feature for formatting letters known as Mail Merge. Once the Address Book data source has been created, the Salutation needs to be set up and written in order to address the person or business the document is meant for. The Mail Merge Wizard provides tools that allow the user to quickly create salutations in only a few short steps.

Before covering salutations, complete **Step 1** through **Step 3** of the Mail Merge Wizard. The following steps outline how this task is done.

Step 1: Select **Create a New Document** from the **Select Starting Document** dialog box.

Step 2: Select **Letter** from the **Select Document Type** dialog box.

Step 3: Select an **Address List** from the **Insert Address Block** dialog box.

After these three steps have been completed, Writer allows the user to create a salutation. A salutation can be created through the **Create a Salutation** dialog box; the steps are outlined below.

Step 1: Check the checkbox next to **This Document Should Contain a Salutation**. Once checked, the fields in the Create a Salutation dialog box will become available.

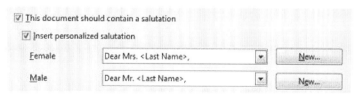

Figure 1

Step 2: If a personal salutation is needed, click the checkbox next to **Insert Personalized Salutation**. If a general salutation is needed, do NOT click the checkbox next to **Insert Personalized Salutation**.

Step 3: Depending on what was selected in **Step 2**, Writer provides options for the user. If the general salutation is selected, the default salutation is "To whom it may concern," and by selecting this, this salutation will be used for all recipients of the mail merge. If a personalized salutation is selected, Writer allows the user to choose a greeting. Next to each gender there is a drop-down menu that has a variety of common salutations.

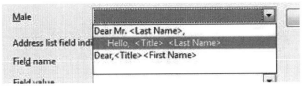

Figure 2

Note – Writer allows the user to create additional customized salutations by clicking **New…**, which is located next to the drop-down menu.

Step 4: Select whether the recipient is male or female. The Wizard's default is "Mr." or male. To indicate that the recipient is female, select the field name and field value under the header "Address list field indicating a female recipient." The most common **Field Name** to use is **Gender**, and the most common **Field Value** to use is **F**. The Mail Merge Wizard will read this code when merging the documents.

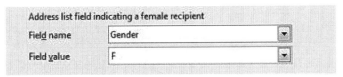

Figure 3

Step 5: Writer allows the user to preview the salutations by scrolling through the documents using the arrows at the bottom of the **Create a Salutation** dialog box. The **Preview Window** allows the user to view the recently created salutations in the documents.

Figure 4

Step 6: Click **Next >>** to move onto the next step in the Mail Merge Wizard.

Adjusting the Page Layout in Mail Merge

After adding different elements to the source document, the Mail Merge Wizard allows the user to adjust the layout. The **Adjust Layout** step, in the Mail Merge Wizard, is split into two portions; the Address Block position, and the Salutation position. Both portions are described below.

Address Block Position – This portion of the dialog box determines where the Address Block is located on the document. The Wizard allows the user to control the position of the Address Block by using the arrows to move the block up and down, or left and right. If the **Align to Text Body** checkbox is checked, the wizard will align the Address Block in the same position as the text of the letter; it will not allow the Address Block to move further to the right or left.

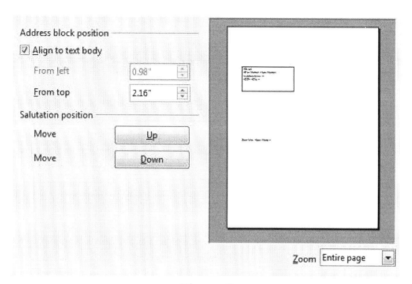

Figure 5

Salutation Position – This portion of the dialog box determines where the Salutation is located on the document. The Salutation's position can only be adjusted up or down, it cannot be adjusted left or right.

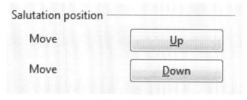

Figure 6

Note – The **Preview Window** in the dialog box allows the user to view how the document looks as modifications are made.

Growth & Assessment

1. How many steps must be completed before a salutation can be created in the Mail Merge Wizard?

2. The checkbox next to This Document Should Contain a Salutation should be checked in order to edit the other fields within the Create a Salutation dialog box.

    a. TRUE

    b. FALSE

3. What is the purpose of the Preview Window?

4. The Salutation position can only be adjusted left or right.

    a. TRUE

    b. FALSE

Section 1.15 – Editing the Mail Merge

Section Objectives:

- Learn how to edit a document in Mail Merge.

- Learn how to personalize a document in Mail Merge.

- Learn how to save, print, and send a document in Mail Merge.

Editing a Document in Mail Merge

The Mail Merge feature in OpenOffice Writer has multiple components. The Address Book data source must be created in order to add the mailing information for a document; the Salutation must be set up and written in order to address the person or business; the document must be saved, printed and sent. This section explains how to add the finishing touches to a document as well as how to save, print, or send the document depending on how the user wants to distribute the document.

Before covering how to edit a document in Mail Merge, complete **Step 1** through **Step 5** of the Mail Merge Wizard. The following steps outline how this task is done.

Step 1: Select **Create a New Document** from the **Select Starting Document** dialog box.

Step 2: Select **Letter** from the **Select Document Type** dialog box.

Step 3: Select an **Address List** from the **Insert Address Block** dialog box.

Step 4: Create a **Salutation** within the letter. This is done through the **Create a Salutation** dialog box.

Step 5: Use the **Adjust Layout** dialog box to determine the position of the address block and salutation within the document.

Once the steps outlined above have been completed, the Mail Merge Wizard allows the user to edit the document. Editing is a crucial step in all writing, especially when the documents contain important information and are sent to multiple recipients. The Mail Merge Wizard's **Edit Document** dialog box makes it easy for users to edit all of the documents in just a few steps.

Before covering the necessary steps, it is important to note the two portions of the **Edit Document** dialog box. Both portions are described below.

Preview: This portion of the dialog box allows users to scroll through the different recipients of the Mail Merge to view how each document will look once it is created.

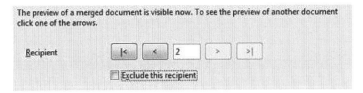

Figure 1

Edit Document: This portion of the dialog box allows the user to edit all of the Mail Merge documents at the same time.

Figure 2

Before viewing the document using the Preview portion, it is important to make any necessary edits. The following steps outline how to edit all of the documents at the same time.

Step 1: Click the **Edit Document...** button on the **Edit Document** dialog box.

Step 2: Once the Mail Merge Wizard shrinks into a smaller window, the user is allowed to make any necessary edits to the source document.

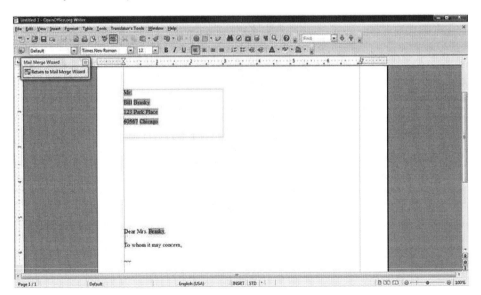

Figure 3

Step 3: After modifying the source document, click the **Return to Mail Merge Wizard** button. This will expand the Mail Merge Wizard window to its original size.

Figure 4

Step 4: Use the arrows, in the Preview portion of the **Edit Document** dialog box, to scroll through the recipients and preview what the documents will look like.

   Note – If a particular address needs to be excluded from the merge, click the checkbox next to **Exclude This Recipient**.

Step 5: After previewing all Mail Merge documents, click **Next** to create them. The Mail Merge Wizard will create a document for each entry in the selected address book and display those documents on the screen.

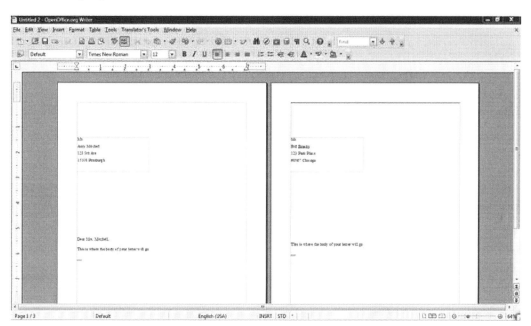

Figure 5

Personalize a Document in Mail Merge

The Mail Merge feature was developed to give users the ability to create multiple copies of the same document without having to type, or copy/paste, the same text numerous times; however, if a user wants to modify a particular recipient's document without altering others, this can be done in the **Personalize the Mail Merge Documents** dialog box. The steps below outline how to use this feature to make changes to individual documents.

Step 1: In the **Personalize the Mail Merge Documents** dialog box, click **Edit Individual Document...**

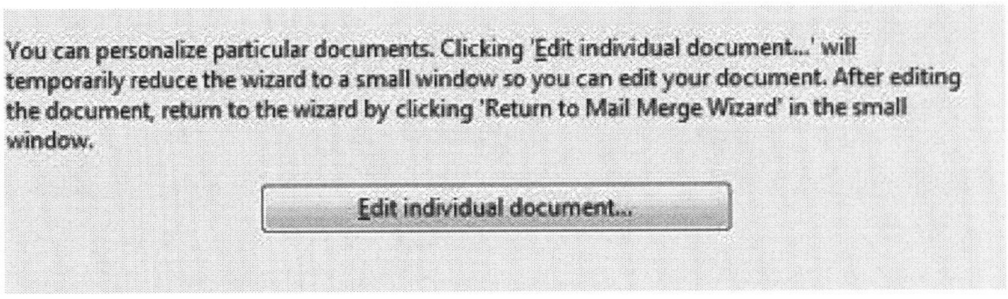

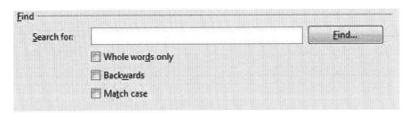

Figure 6

Step 2: Once the Mail Merge Wizard window shrinks, make all necessary modifications.

Step 3: After modifications have been made, click **Return to Mail Merge Wizard**. This will expand the Mail Merge Wizard to its original size.

Step 4: If the modifications to the document(s) are acceptable, click **Next >>**. This will direct the user to the final step of the Mail Merge Wizard.

Note – The **Personalize the Mail Merge Documents** dialog box also contains a **Search** feature that allows the user to find a particular document. This feature is helpful when selecting specific recipients out of a large address book.

Figure 7

Saving, Printing, or Sending a Document in Mail Merge

The final step in the Mail Merge Wizard is arguably the most important. All of the work that has been done to reach this final step would be for nothing if there wasn't a way to distribute the documents to the necessary recipients. The **Save, Print or Send the Document** dialog box provides the user with four options which are described below.

Save Starting Document – This option saves the original document that was created before merging the addresses.

Save Merged Document – This option allows the user to save all of the merged documents into a single document, or into individual documents for each recipient.

Print Merged Document – This option allows the user to print all of the merged documents, or select particular documents to print.

Send Merged Document as E-Mail – This option has the ability to send the Mail Merged documents via e-mail to all of the recipients in the address book, or only to selected recipients.

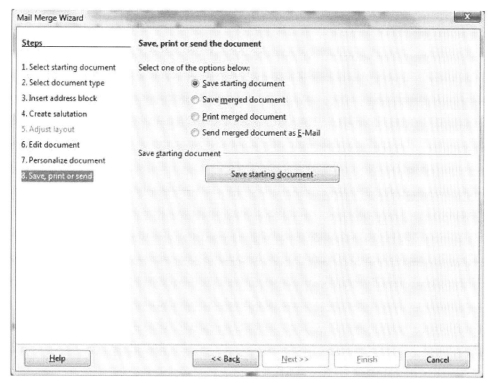

Figure 8

Once a distribution method is selected, click **Finish** and the Mail Merge Wizard will close.

Growth & Assessment

1. Mail Merge in Writer has many components.

    a. TRUE

    b. FALSE

2. What are the two portions of the Edit Document dialog box?

3. What is the purpose of the search feature in the Personalize the Mail Merge Documents dialog box?

4. How many options are listed in the Save, Print or Send the Document dialog box?

Unit Two

Section 2.1 – Editing a Writer Document   68

Section 2.2 – Checking Spelling and Grammar   72

Section 2.3 – Inserting Page Numbers   78

Section 2.4 – Inserting the Date and Time   82

Section 2.5 – The Thesaurus, Dictionary, and Word Count   89

Section 2.6 – Using the Translator's Tools   97

Section 2.7 – Adding a Hyperlink to the Document   101

Section 2.8 – Creating an Outline   107

Section 2.9 – Finding and Replacing Text   112

Section 2.10 – Using AutoCorrect   117

Section 2.11 – Creating a Table   121

Section 2.12 – Using AutoText   125

Section 2.13 – Formatting Tables   129

Section 2.14 – Working with Table Data   134

Section 2.15 – Using Columns to Present Text   138

Section 2.1 – Editing a Writer Document

Section Objective:

- Learn how to edit a document in Writer.

Editing a Document in Writer

OpenOffice Writer offers many options for editing the text within a document. The three most often used options for editing the text within a document are Cut, Paste, and Copy. Before covering these editing options, two features need to be introduced.

- **Clipboard** – The clipboard is a feature in Writer where temporary information is stored for easy retrieval.
- **Highlighting** – Highlighting is a process of using the cursor to select a portion of the text. To highlight something, begin by positioning the cursor at the beginning of the desired text. Then, click and hold down the left mouse key and drag the cursor to the end of the text, and once the entire text is selected, release the mouse key. The text will now be highlighted.

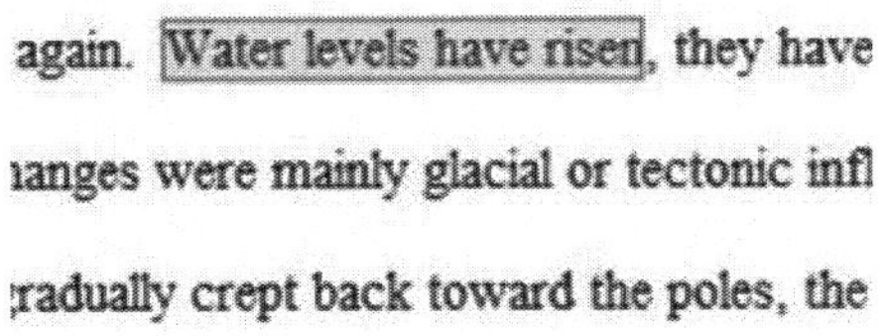

again. Water levels have risen, they have
ıanges were mainly glacial or tectonic infl
;radually crept back toward the poles, the

Figure 1

Using Cut, Copy, and Paste

The **Cut** tool is used to "cut out" a specific portion of the text. This is done for one of two reasons. Either a portion of text is not needed, or a portion is needed elsewhere, and will be used within another section of the text.

Steps for Using Cut:

Step 1: Open Writer and create a new document. Choose a familiar topic and write three sentences about the topic. Once written, highlight the first sentence.

This is example one.
This is example two.
This is example three.

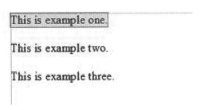

Figure 2

Step 2: Click **Edit**, located on the **Menu** Bar.

Step 3: Within the Edit drop-down menu, select **Cut**. This will remove the highlighted sentence from the beginning of the text.

   Note – The keyboard shortcut **CTRL + X** will also *Cut* the highlighted text.

Step 4: Now that the text has been cut, it is ready to me moved. Place the cursor at the end of the third sentence. From the Edit drop-down menu, select **Paste**. The first sentence will be pasted at the end of the third sentence.

   Note – The keyboard shortcut **CTRL + V** will also *Paste* the highlighted text.

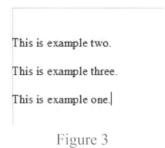

Figure 3

Steps for Using Copy:

The **Copy** tool is used to repeat particular sections from the text. Copied text will be stored on the clipboard. Unlike the Cut tool, Copy will not remove the highlighted text.

Step 1: Using the same document, highlight the first sentence.

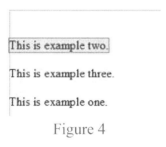

Figure 4

Step 2: Click **Edit**, located on Menu Bar.

Step 3: From the Edit drop-down menu, select **Copy**. This will copy the highlighted sentence, but leave the sentence in its original form.

   Note – The keyboard shortcut **CTRL + C** will also *Copy* the highlighted text.

Step 4: Now that the text has been copied, it is ready to me moved. Place the cursor at the end of the third sentence. From the Edit drop-down menu, select **Paste**. The first sentence will be pasted at the end of the third sentence.

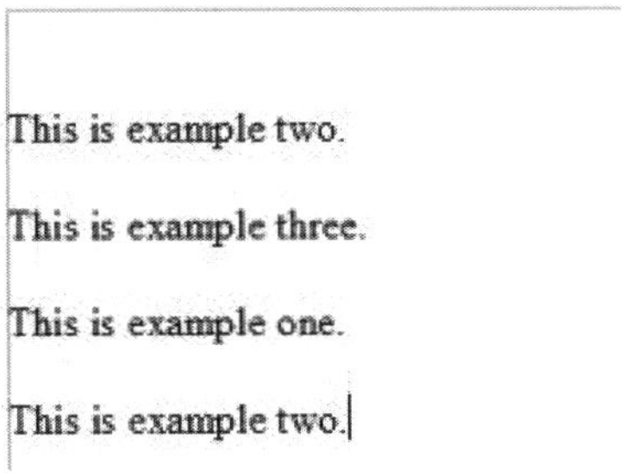

> This is example two.
>
> This is example three.
>
> This is example one.
>
> This is example two.

Figure 5

Moving Text without Using Cut

Step 1: Using the same document, highlight the first sentence.

Step 2: With the left mouse button, click and hold the highlighted text and drag it to the end of the last sentence.

> **Note** – The insertion line shows where the text will be placed.

> This is example two.

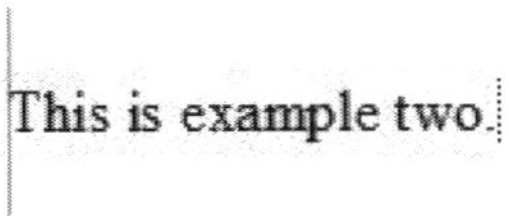

Figure 6

Step 3: Release the left mouse button. The highlighted text will be placed at the end of the third sentence.

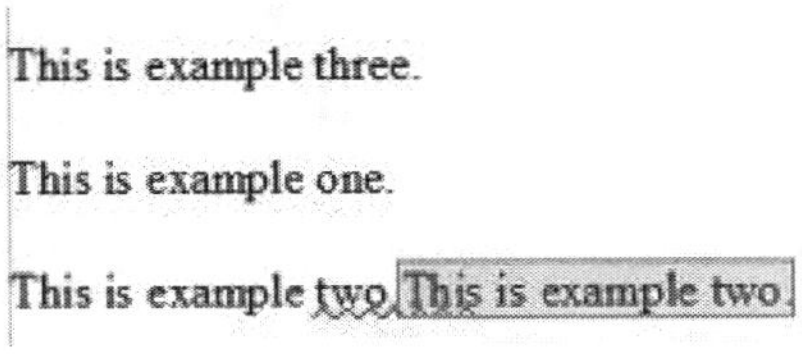

> This is example three.
>
> This is example one.
>
> This is example two. This is example two.

Figure 7

Copying Text without Using the Clipboard

Step 1: Using the same document, highlight the first sentence.

Step 2: Press and hold the **CTRL** key, located on the keyboard.

Step 3: While holding the **CTRL** key, use the left mouse button to click and drag the highlighted text to the end of the last sentence.

Step 4: Release the left mouse button and **CTRL**. The highlighted text will be placed at the end of the third sentence.

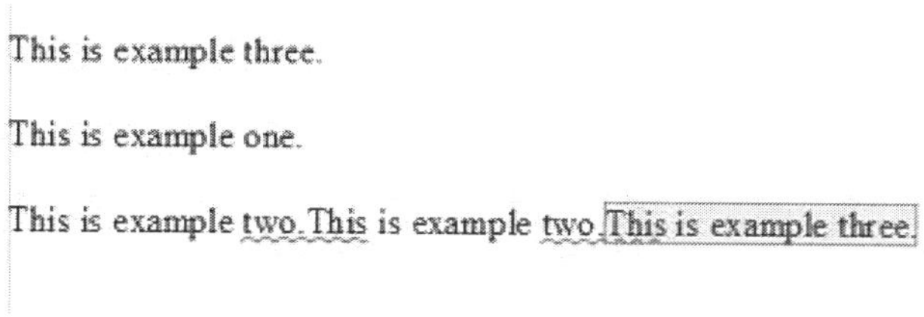

> This is example three.
>
> This is example one.
>
> This is example two. This is example two. This is example three.

Figure 8

Growth & Assessment

1. What is the purpose of the clipboard in Writer?

2. Cut is used to copy a specific section of text within a document.

    a. TRUE

    b. FALSE

3. What is the Cut keyboard shortcut?

4. What is the Copy keyboard shortcut?

Section 2.2 – Checking Spelling and Grammar

Section Objective:

- Learn how to check spelling and grammar.

Correcting Misspelled Words

One of the most important features found within OpenOffice Writer is the Spelling and Grammar tool. This tool allows users to correct misspelled words and other grammatical errors within a document. Writer uses a built-in dictionary to reference unfamiliar words, and when a misspelled word has been typed in a document, Writer will underline the word with a red line.

Writer offers two options to correct a misspelled word. The first option is through the **Quick Menu**. The second option is through the **Spelling and Grammar** tool found on the Menu Bar.

The Quick Menu

Step 1: Open a new Writer document. Type the word "**Missspellledd.**" A wavy red line will appear under the word.

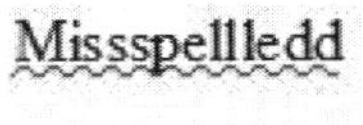

Missspellledd

Figure 1

The Quick Menu not only allows the user to correct a misspelled word, it also offers several other important options. The options are listed below.

- **Spelling Suggestions** – Gives suggestions for correcting the misspelled word.

- **Ignore** – Ignores that instance of the word.

- **Ignore All** – Ignores that word and every other instance of that word.

- **Add** – Adds the word to the dictionary.

- **AutoCorrect** – Provides word choices for the AutoCorrect function.

- **Spelling and Grammar** – Opens the Spelling and Grammar dialog box.

Step 2: **Right-click** the misspelled word. The **Quick Menu** will appear. Notice the top section of the Quick Menu offers suggestions for the misspelled word. Choose the word that was originally meant when the text was entered.

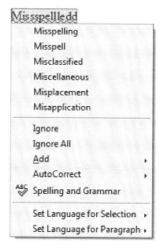

Figure 2

The Spelling and Grammar Tool

Step 1: Using the same document, click **Tools**, located on the Menu Bar.

Step 2: From the Tools drop-down menu, select **Spelling and Grammar…**. The Spelling and Grammar dialog box will appear.

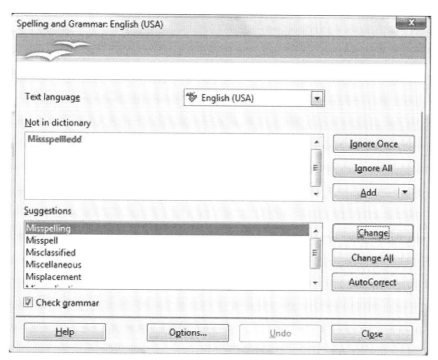

Figure 3

Step 3: Choose the correct version of the misspelled word.

73

Correcting Grammar

Writer also allows the user to correct grammar using a feature called the **Language Tool**; however, most versions of OpenOffice Writer do not come equipped with this feature. To download this feature from the internet, follow the steps below.

Step 1: Go to the following link: *http://extensions.services.openoffice.org/project/languagetool*

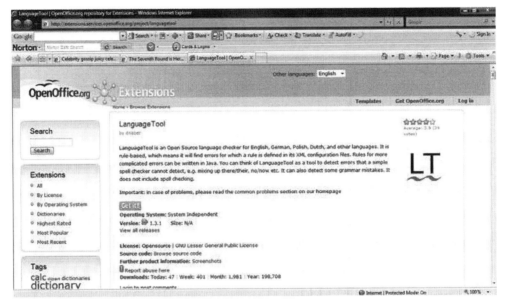

Figure 4

Step 2: The OpenOffice Language Tool page will appear. Click the **Get it!** button in the middle of the page. The Download Page will appear.

Figure 5

Step 3: Click **Manual Download**. The download will begin.

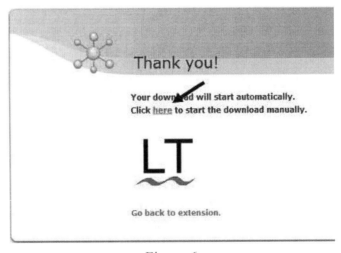

Figure 6

Step 4: When prompted, click **Open** on the File Download window.

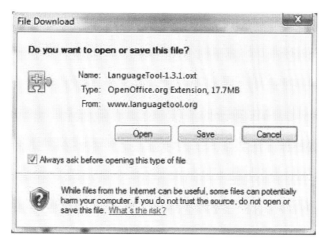

Figure 7

Step 5: The next prompt will ask the user to verify the installation of the **Language Tool**. Click **OK** and then click **Accept** to accept the license agreement.

Figure 8

Step 6: When the **Extension Manager** window appears showing that the tool has been added to Writer, click **Close**. The Language Tool has now been installed and is ready to use.

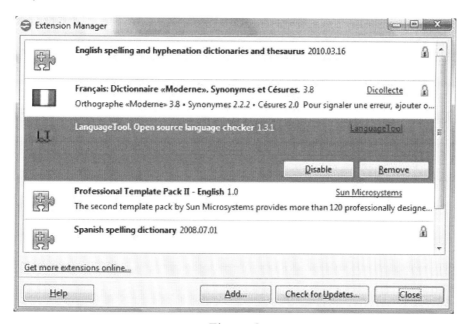

Figure 9

75

Using the Language Tool

Similar to correcting misspelled words, correcting grammar can be done in one of two ways. The first option is to use the **Quick Menu**. The second option is to go through the **Spelling and Grammar** tool found on the Menu Bar.

The Quick Menu

Step 1: Open a new Writer document. Type the sentence "**This is an bad sentence.**" Notice the wavy blue line under the word "**an**."

This is an bad sentence.

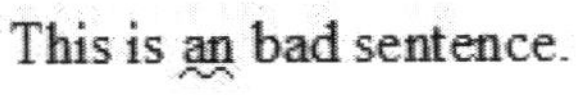

Figure 10

Step 2: **Right-click** the underlined word. The **Quick Menu** will appear. Choose the correct use of the word from the grammar suggestions.

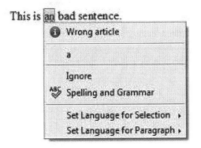

Figure 11

The Spelling and Grammar Tool

Step 1: Similar to the steps above, open a new Writer document and type the same sentence into the document. Once again, the wavy blue line under the word "**an**" will appear.

Step 2: Click **Tools**, located on the **Menu** Bar.

Step 3: From the Tools drop-down menu, click **Language Tool** and then select **Check Text**. The **Spelling and Grammar** dialog box will appear.

Figure 12

Step 4: Writer will suggest a replacement word, or letter, under **Suggestions**. Select the preferred suggestion, and then click **Change**.

Step 5: When finished, click **Close** to exit the Spelling and Grammar dialog box.

Growth & Assessment

1. The dictionary in Writer uses a solid blue line to let the user know a word is misspelled.

    a. TRUE

    b. FALSE

2. What are the two ways to correct a misspelled word in Writer?

3. Within the Quick Menu, what choice *ignores the selected word and all instances of the word*?

4. Writer comes ready with the Language Tool.

    a. TRUE

    b. FALSE

Section 2.3 – Inserting Page Numbers

Section Objective:

- Learn how to insert page numbers into a document.

Page Numbers in Writer

OpenOffice Writer has many features that allow the user to customize a document in many ways. One such feature is the option to insert a page number. Page numbers add a professional look, as well as a way for others reading the document to quickly reference specific pages. Once inserted, the page numbers are found along the margins of the document.

Before covering the steps needed to add page numbers to a document, Writer has two features that should be defined: **Header** and **Footer**

- **Header** – The Header is the additional information displayed in the top margin of the document. This information within the header will be displayed on all pages of the document.

- **Footer** – The Footer is the additional information displayed in the bottom margin of the document. Like the header, this information will be displayed on all pages of the document.

Inserting Page Numbers

Step 1: Open a previously saved Writer document that is multiple pages in length.

Step 2: Click **Insert**, located on the Menu Bar.

Step 3: From the Insert drop-down menu, select **Footer** and then click **Default**. A blank Footer will be created at the bottom of the page, below the text.

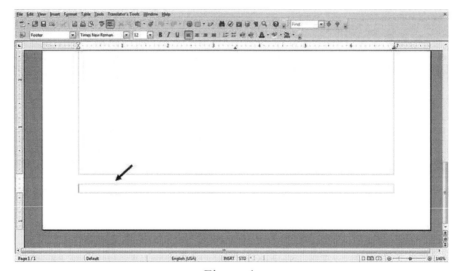

Figure 1

Step 4: Click anywhere inside the blank Footer.

Step 5: Once the insertion point is placed in the blank footer, click **Insert** on the Menu Bar.

Step 6: From the Insert drop-down menu, select **Fields** and then click **Page Number**. Page numbers will be inserted into the footer of the document.

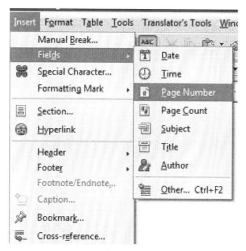

Figure 2

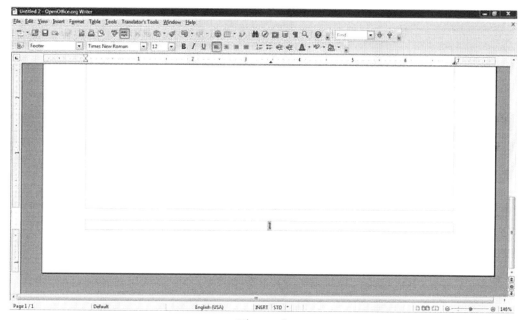

Figure 3

Note – The steps above also apply to the Header; however, in **Step 3** select **Header** instead of selecting **Footer**.

Formatting Page Numbers

Now that the document pages have been number, additional formatting changes may still be needed before the document can be finalized. The following steps outline how to format page numbers in Writer.

Step 1: Return to the first page of the document. Using the left mouse button, highlight the page number.

Step 2: Right-click the highlighted page number and select **Fields…**. The **Edit Fields: Document** dialog box will appear.

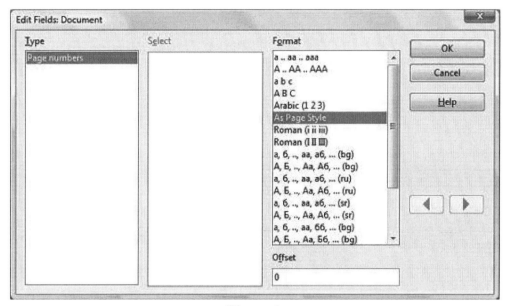

Figure 4

Note – The **Edit Fields: Document** dialog box shows all of the different formatting options for page numbers. Different documents will require different page number formats.

Step 3: Within the **Edit Fields: Document** dialog box, select the **Roman (i ii iii)** Format.

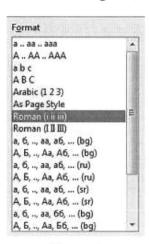

Figure 5

Step 4: After selecting the **Roman (i ii iii)** Format option, click **OK**. The pages will now use a Roman numeral style of numbering.

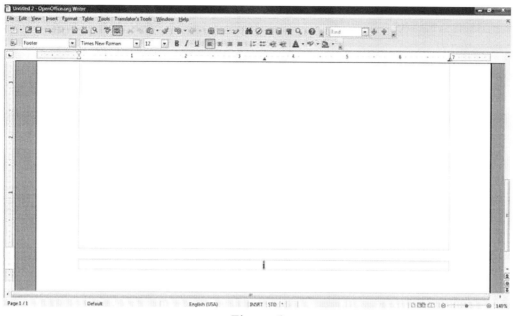

Figure 6

Growth & Assessment

1. Where can page numbers be inserted within a document in Writer?

2. Where is the Footer located in a document?

3. Page numbers can also be inserted at the top of the document, above the text.

    a. TRUE

    b. FALSE

4. What is an example of a page number format found in Writer?

Section 2.4 – Inserting the Date and Time

Section Objective:

- Learn how to insert the date and time.

Date and Time in Writer

OpenOffice Writer has many format features that allow the user to personalize a document for a specific purpose. One such feature is the ability to insert the current date and time within a document. This feature is useful when composing letters or memos, or any other type of document that requires the date and time.

Inserting the Current Date

Step 1: Open a new Writer document.

Step 2: Click **Insert**, located on the Menu Bar.

Step 3: From the Insert drop-down menu, select **Fields**.

Step 4: Within **Fields**, select **Date**. The current date will be inserted into the document.

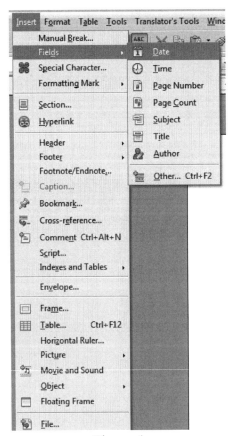

Figure 1

Figure 2

Formatting the Current Date

In Writer, the user has the ability to choose which way the inserted date is displayed. These formatting options can be accessed through the **Edit Fields: Document** dialog box. The steps below outline how this is done.

Step 1: **Right-click** the on inserted date and select **Fields…**. The **Edit Fields: Document** dialog box will appear.

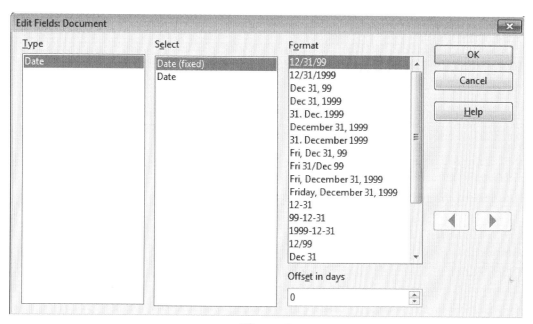

Figure 3

Step 2: Select the preferred date format and click **OK**. The new date format will be applied to the inserted date.

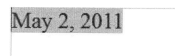

Figure 4

Inserting the Current Time

In some instances, the user may want to insert the current time within a document. This is done similarly to inserting the current date. The steps below outline how this is done.

Step 1: Using the same document, click **Insert** on the Menu Bar.

Step 2: From the Insert drop-down menu, select **Fields**.

Step 3: Within **Fields**, select **Time**. The current time will be inserted into the document.

Figure 5

Formatting the Current Time

In Writer, the user also has the ability to choose which way the inserted time is displayed within the document. These formatting options can be accessed through the **Edit Fields: Document** dialog box. The steps below outline how this is done.

Step 1: **Right-click** the on inserted time and select **Fields…**. The **Edit Fields: Document** dialog box will appear.

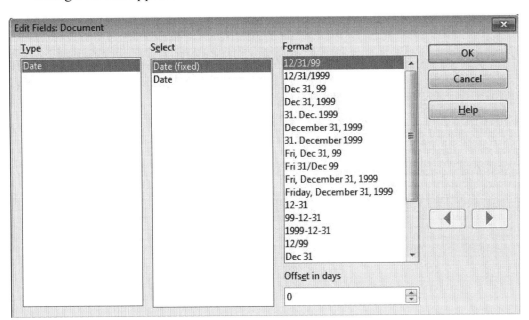

Figure 3

Step 2: Select the preferred time format and click **OK**. The new time format will be applied to the inserted time.

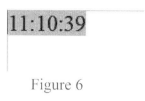

Figure 6

Entering a Time Stamp

An instance may occur when a specific document change needs its own specific date and time. This feature is called a **Time Stamp**. Time stamps are often used in college settings to show a professor when a specific portion of a paper or assignment has been replaced or edited. The following steps outline how to insert a time stamp within a document.

Step 1: Using the same document as above, place the cursor below the previously inserted date and time.

Step 3: Click **Insert**, located on the Menu Bar.

Step 4: From the Insert drop-down menu, select **Fields**.

Step 5: Within Fields, select **Other…**. The **Edit Fields: Document** dialog box will appear.

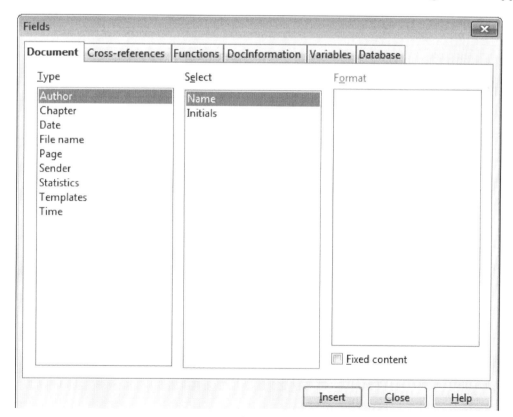

Figure 7

Step 6: Select the **DocInformation** tab. The **Edit Fields: DocInformation** dialog box will appear.

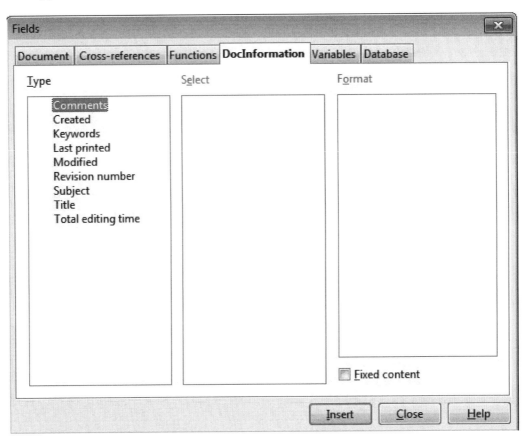

Figure 8

Step 7: In the **Type** selection window, choose **Modified**.

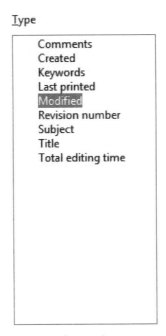

Figure 9

Step 8: In the **Select** selection window, choose **Time**.

Figure 10

Step 7: In the **Format** selection window, choose the preferred time format.

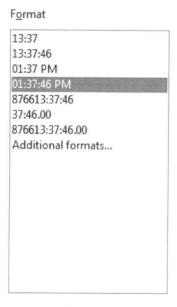

Figure 11

Step 8: Click **Insert**, and then click **Close**. A time stamp will be added to the document.

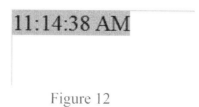

Figure 12

Step 9: Once the time stamp has been added to the document, save the document in a separate folder.

Note – It is important to save the recently changed document to a separate folder so that it can be referenced later. If the same document is updated throughout the editing process and a new time stamp in added every time, the user will have no way of going back and identifying the date and time at which the document was altered.

Growth & Assessment

1. Users are unable to insert date and time within a Writer document.

    a. TRUE

    b. FALSE

2. What is a time stamp?

3. What type of documents may require a date or time?

Section 2.5 – The Thesaurus, Dictionary, and Word Count

Section Objectives:

- Learn how to use the Thesaurus.

- Learn how to use the Dictionary.

- Learn how to view the Word Count.

Using Thesaurus in Writer

OpenOffice Writer offers many features and tools. One important tool is the **Thesaurus**. The Thesaurus is used to look up alternative words with similar meanings, called **synonyms**. This is important in writing because repetition of the same word can bore the audience. The following steps outline how to use the Thesaurus tool in Writer.

Step 1: Create a new Writer document. Type a word into the document. For this example, use the word "fun." Once the word has been typed into the document, highlight the word.

Step 2: Click **Tools**, located on the Menu Bar.

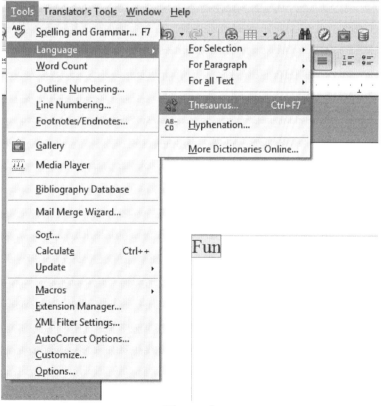

Figure 1

Step 3: From the Tools drop-down menu, select **Language** and then click **Thesaurus**. The **Thesaurus** dialog box will appear.

Step 4: The highlighted word, "Fun," is shown in the upper left-hand side of the dialog box under **Current word**. Below "Fun" is a list of the word's synonyms.

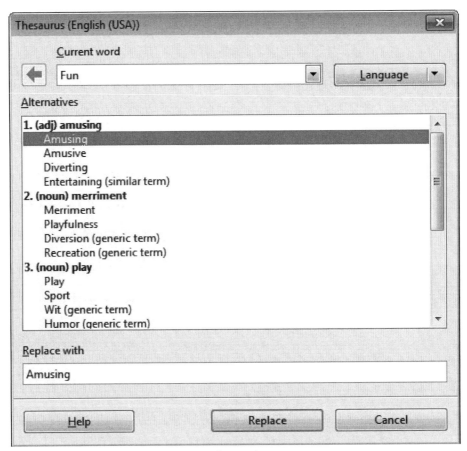

Figure 2

Step 4: Select "**Amusing**" from the list of synonyms and then click **Replace**. The word "Amusing" will replace the word "Fun" in the document.

Using the Dictionary in Writer

Another useful tool in Writer is the dictionary tool, called **Translator's Tools**. The **Translator's Tools** allows the user to look up definitions of unfamiliar words. Some versions of Writer may not come equipped with the **Translator's Tools**. The following steps outline how to download the Translator Tools from the internet.

Note – If the version of Writer being used has the Translator's Tools, skip the following steps.

Downloading the Translator's Tool

Step 1: Go to the following link: *http://extensions.services.openoffice.org/en/project/translatortools*

Step 2: The OpenOffice Translator's Tools page will appear. Click the **Get it!** button in the middle of the page. The Download Page will appear.

Figure 3

Step 3: Click **Manual Download**. The download will begin.

Figure 4

Step 4: When prompted, click the **Open** button on the File Download window.

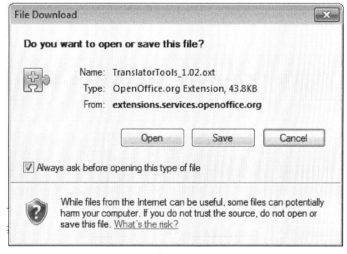

Figure 5

Step 5: The next prompt will ask the user to verify the installation of the **Translator's Tools**. Click **OK**, and then click **Accept** to accept the license agreement.

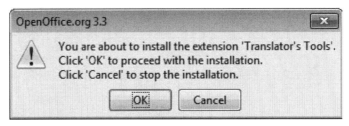

Figure 6

Step 6: Next, the **Extension Manager** window will appear. This window will show that the Translator's Tools has been added to Writer. After confirming that the tool has been installed, click **Close**.

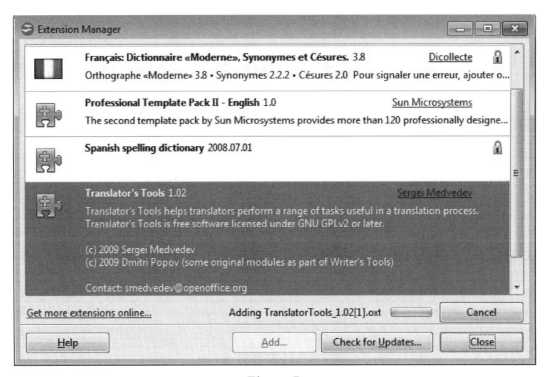

Figure 7

Using the Translator's Tool

Note – Using the Translator's Tools requires access to the internet.

Step 1: Open a new Writer document. For this exercise, type the word "Plethora" into the document. After the text has been entered, use the left mouse button to highlight the word.

Step 2: From the Menu Bar, select **Translator's Tools** and then click **Google Translate**. The **Google Translate** dialog box will appear.

Figure 8

Step 3: Under **Translate from:**, select **English** and under **Mode,** select **Word find**.

Figure 9

Step 4: After selecting the options in **Step 4**, click **Translate**. The **Dictionary** page will appear. The definition of the word highlighted in **Step 1** (Plethora) will be displayed on this page.

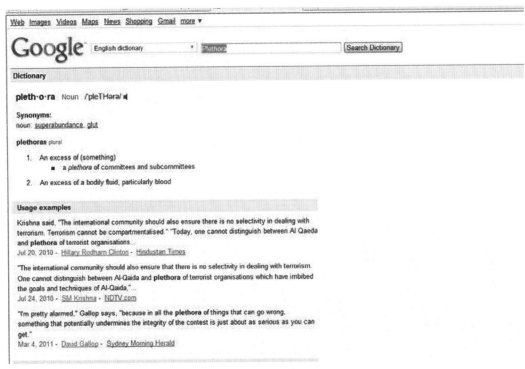

Figure 10

Using Word Count in Writer

Writer's **Word Count** keeps track of the number of words and characters used in a document. This is an important tool when writing research papers and other assignments that require a minimum, and/or maximum number of words. The following steps explain how to use this tool.

Step 1: Open a previously saved Writer document and click **Tools,** which is located on the Menu Bar.

Step 2: Within the Tools drop-down menu, select **Word Count**.

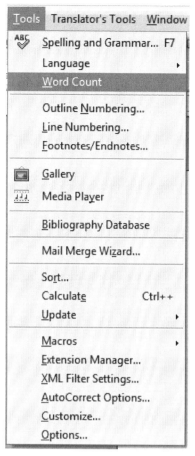

Figure 11

Step 3: The **Word Count** dialog box will appear. Here, the user can view the word count for the entire document.

> **Note** – If text was selected prior to opening the word count, the word count will display the number of words in the selected text and the total word count for the document.

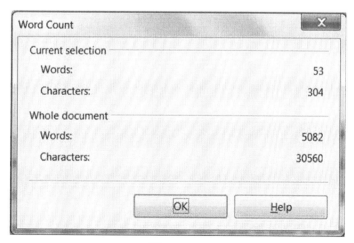

Figure 12

Growth & Assessment

1. Use the Thesaurus feature to find the first three synonyms of the word "plethora."

2. How would a user navigate to the Thesaurus?

3. The Translator's Tool is used to find synonyms.

    a. TRUE

    b. FALSE

4. What is the purpose of the Word Count tool?

Section 2.6 – Using the Translator's Tools

Section Objective:

- Learn how to use the Translator's Tools feature.

Using Translator's Tools in Writer

The **Translator's Tools** in OpenOffice Writer is an easy-to-use tool that allows the user to translate text from one language to another. The Translator's Tools saves time by providing everything the user needs to translate the text, in one location. Writer may not come equipped with the **Translator's Tools;** if this is the case, the following steps outline how to download the Translator's Tools from the internet.

Note – If the version of Writer being used has the Translator's Tools, skip the following steps.

Downloading the Translator's Tools

Step 1: Go to the following link: *http://extensions.services.openoffice.org/en/project/translatortools*

Step 2: The OpenOffice Translator's Tools page will appear. Click the **Get it!** button in the middle of the page. The Download Page will appear.

Figure 1

Step 3: Click **Manual Download**. The download will begin.

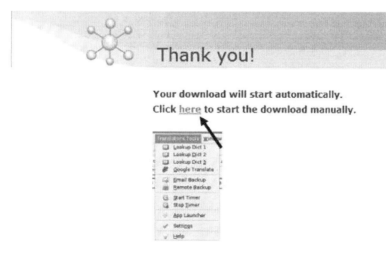

Figure 2

Step 4: When prompted, click the **Open** button on the File Download window.

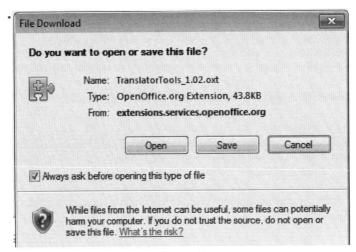

Figure 3

Step 5: The next prompt will ask the user to verify the installation of the **Translator's Tools**. Click **OK**, and then click **Accept** to accept the license agreement.

Figure 4

Step 6: Next, the **Extension Manager** window will appear. This window will show that the Translator's Tools has been added to Writer. After confirming that the tool has been installed, click **Close**.

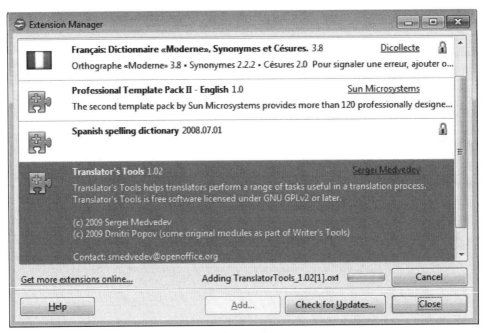

Figure 5

Translating Text with the Translator's Tools

Note – Using the Translator's Tools requires access to the internet.

Step 1: Create a new Writer document and type a few sentences into the document.

Step 2: Highlight the text using the left mouse button.

Step 3: From the drop-down Menu Bar, select **Translator's Tools** and then click **Google Translate**. The **Google Translate** dialog box will appear.

Step 4: Select the language that the text is translating from, **English**, and the preferred language the text will be translated to.

Figure 6

Step 6: Click **Translate**. The Translate page will appear with the selected text translated into the language specified in **Step 4**.

Figure 7

Step 7: Copy the translated text from the Translate page and **Paste** it into the Writer document.

Growth & Assessment

1. What is the tool used in Writer to translate text from one language to another?

2. The Translator's Tools may need to be downloaded before using the translate feature.

    a. TRUE

    b. FALSE

3. Which option should be selected under Mode, within the Google Translate dialog box, in order to properly translate the selected text?

Section 2.7 – Adding a Hyperlink to the Document

Section Objective:

- Learn how to add Hyperlinks to a document.

Using Hyperlinks in Writer

OpenOffice Writer allows the user to set up hyperlinks within a document. A hyperlink is a connection between a particular section of a document, such as a word or an image, and a target location. The target location can be a website, another file, or a specific place within the current document. The following steps will explain how to use hyperlinks to connect to both outside locations, such as websites, and to locations within the document.

Using Hyperlinks to Connect to the Internet

Using a hyperlink to connect to the internet is a way to attach additional information to a document without having to directly incorporate it into the text. The following steps outline how to hyperlink a portion of text to a website.

Note – Internet access is required for this type of hyperlink.

Step 1: Open an existing Writer document with multiple pages.

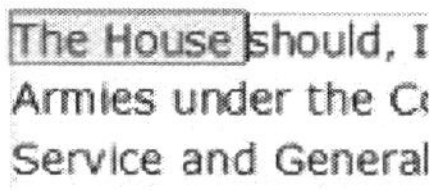

Figure 1

Step 2: Highlight the specific text to hyperlink.

Step 3: Click **Insert**, located on the Menu Bar.

Step 4: From the Insert drop-down menu, select **Hyperlink**. The **Hyperlink** dialog box will appear.

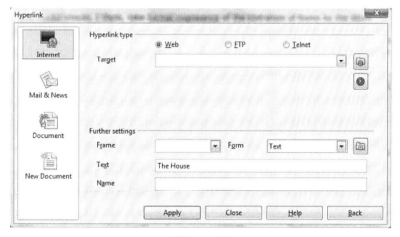

Figure 2

Step 5: Under **Hyperlink type**, click the radio button next to **Web.**

Step 4: Type in the desired website address.

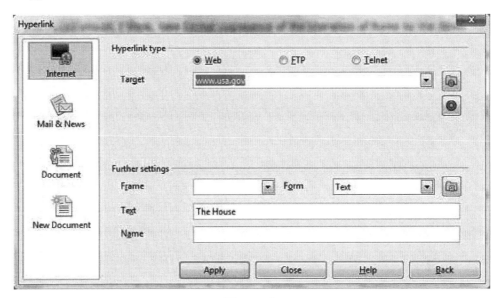

Figure 3

Step 5: The text selected to be hyperlinked is displayed under the **Further Settings** portion of the **Hyperlink** dialog box. Make any needed changes to the selected text in the **Text** textbox.

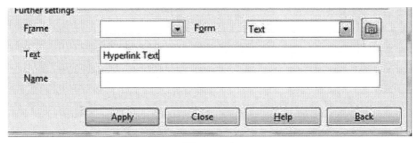

Figure 4

Step 6: Once finished, click **Apply**, and then click **Close**. The highlighted text is now a hyperlink to the website address specified in **Step 4**.

Note – Once the hyperlink has been set up, the hyperlinked text within the document will be underlined and colored blue.

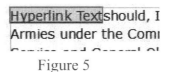

Figure 5

Using Hyperlinks to Connect to Different Locations within the Document

As stated above, Writer allows users to create hyperlinks that connect to different locations within the same document. This can be done by using the **Bookmark** feature. A bookmark is a location, or selection of text, within a document that is named for reference purposes. Bookmarks identify a location within the document that users can link to. In order to create this link, the user must first create a bookmark to identify the hyperlink's destination, and then add a hyperlink to the selected text, which will connect the user to the bookmark. The following steps outline this two-step process.

Creating the Bookmark

Step 1: Open an existing Writer document with multiple pages.

Step 2: Highlight the desired text, or document location, the user will be directed to once clicking on the hyperlink.

Step 3: Click **Insert**, located on the Menu Bar.

Step 4: From the Insert drop-down menu, select **Bookmark**. The **Bookmark** dialog box will appear.

Figure 6

Step 5: Under **Bookmarks**, enter the desired bookmark name and click **OK**. This will create the bookmark which will be used when applying the hyperlink (see below).

Note – Bookmark names must begin with a letter.

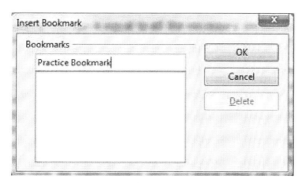

Figure 7

Creating the Hyperlink

Step 1: Highlight the specific text to hyperlink.

Step 2: Click **Insert**, located on the Menu Bar.

Step 3: Within the Insert drop-down menu, select **Hyperlink**. The **Hyperlink** dialog box will appear.

Step 4: Click the **Document** link in the left-hand window pane of the **Hyperlink** dialog box.

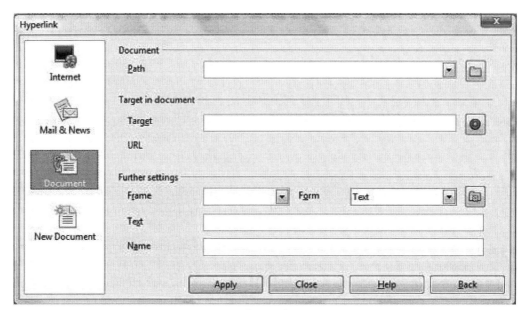

Figure 8

Step 5: In the **Target in document** portion of the window, click the **bull's-eye** icon. The **Target in document** pop-up window will appear.

Figure 9

Step 6: Click on the plus sign next to the **Bookmarks** heading to expand the list of available bookmarks.

Figure 10

Step 7: Select the name of the bookmark previously created and click **Apply**. The bookmark will be added to the **Hyperlink** dialog box.

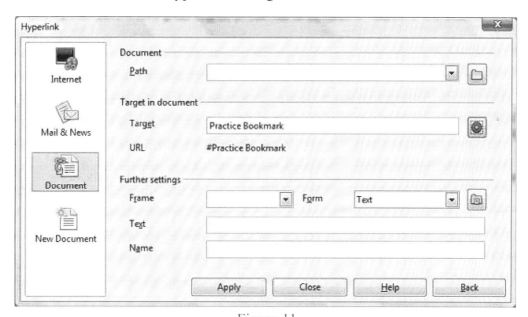

Figure 11

Step 8: The text selected to be hyperlinked is displayed under the **Further settings** portion of the **Hyperlink** dialog box. Make any needed changes to the selected text in the **Text** textbox.

Step 9: Once finished, click **Apply**, and then click **Close**. The highlighted text is now a hyperlink to the bookmark which was created earlier.

105

Deleting Hyperlinks

Writer allows users to easily delete unwanted hyperlinks. The following steps outline how this is done.

Step 1: Highlight the hyperlink within the text.

Step 2: **Right-click** the highlighted hyperlink.

Step 3: Select **Remove Hyperlink**. The hyperlink will then be removed from the selected text.

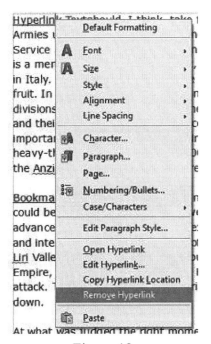

Figure 12

Growth & Assessment

1. What is the purpose of a hyperlink in Writer?

2. What are the two ways to hyperlink in a document?

3. A bookmark allows the user to select and name specific sections of a document.

    a. TRUE

    b. FALSE

4. Explain how to delete a hyperlink within a document.

Section 2.8 – Creating an Outline

Section Objective:

- Learn how to create an outline.

Outlines

Organizing the ideas and thoughts that go into writing a document can be difficult. This is why writers use outlines to help themselves plan their material before beginning a new piece of writing. OpenOffice Writer offers default outlines to help with this process.

Bullets and Numbering

Writer's default outlines are accessed through the **Bullets and Numbering...** tool. The following steps explain how to access this tool and use it to create an outline.

Adding a Default Outline

Step 1: Create a new Writer document.

Step 2: Click **Format**, located on the **Menu** Bar.

Step 3: From the Format drop-down menu, select **Bullets and Numbering...**. The **Bullets and Numbering** dialog box will appear.

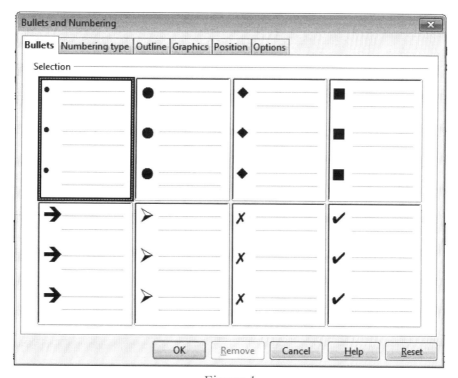

Figure 1

Step 4: From the **Bullets and Numbering** dialog box, select the **Outline** tab.

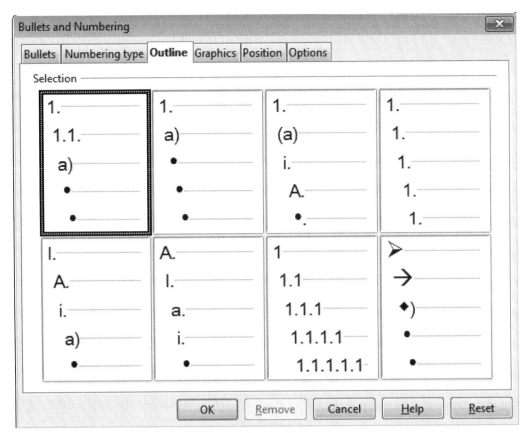

Figure 2

Step 5: Select the preferred outline style. For the purpose of this example, select the style shown in the image below, and click **OK**.

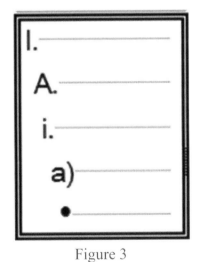

Figure 3

Step 6: The Roman numeral "**I.**" appears in the document. Type "**Item 1.**"

> I.   Item 1

Figure 4

Step 7: Press **Enter**. A new number appears at the same outline level. Continue typing "**Item 2**" **(Enter)**... "**Item 3**" **(Enter)**... "**Item 4**" **(Enter)**... "**Item 5**" and then stop. There are now five items within the outline.

> I.   Item 1
> II.   Item 2
> III.   Item 3
> IV.   Item 4
> V.   Item 5

Figure 5

Customizing an Outline

Once the default outline has been created, the user has the ability to customize the outline by selecting a preferred format and adding or deleting levels. The user must first select the format because once levels are added or deleted the outline automatically adjusts based on the format selected. The following steps outline how this is done.

Note – Before completing the steps below, the user must first select a preferred format.

Step 1: Using the same document, place the cursor directly after "**Item 4.**"

Step 2: Press **Enter**. A new level is added to the outline. In the new level, type "**New Item 4.**"

> I.   Item 1
> II.   Item 2
> III.   Item 3
> IV.   Item 4
> V.   New Item 4
> VI.   Item 5

Figure 6

Step 3: Highlight "**Item 4**."

Step 4: Press **Delete**. Once deleted, "**New Item 4**" will replace the level where "**Item 4**" was previously placed.

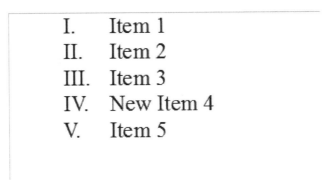

Figure 7

Promoting and Demoting

Another feature of the Bullets and Numbering tool are **Promote** and **Demote**. Promote shifts a line of the outline to the left, while Demote shifts a line of text to the right. The following steps summarize how to **Demote** and **Promote** a line of text within an outline.

How to Demote

Step 1: Using the same document, place the cursor directly after "**Item 3**."

Step 2: Select **Demote One Level with Subpoints** from the **Bullets and Number** tools menu. Once selected, the line of text will be demoted to the next level of the outline.

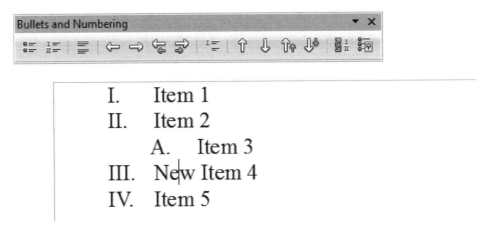

Figure 8

110

How to Promote

Step 1: Using the same document, place the cursor directly after "**Item 4**."

Step 2: Select **Promote One Level with Subpoints** from the **Bullets and Number** tools menu. Once selected, the line of text will be promoted to the next level of the outline.

Growth & Assessment

1. What is the purpose of an outline?

2. Where are default outlines found in Writer?

3. What does it mean to Promote and Demote a line?

Section 2.9 – Finding and Replacing Text

Section Objective:

- Learn how to find and replace text.

Finding Text

OpenOffice Writer offers a way to find specific text within a document. The **Find & Replace** tool allows users to locate specific words or phrases within a document. This is a helpful alternative to searching through larger documents for only a few words or phrases. The following steps outline how to use the **Find & Replace** tool in Writer.

Step 1: Open a previously saved Writer document. Make sure the document is at least a page in length.

Step 2: Click **Edit**, located on the Menu Bar.

Step 3: From the Edit drop-down menu, select **Find & Replace**. The **Find & Replace** dialog box will appear.

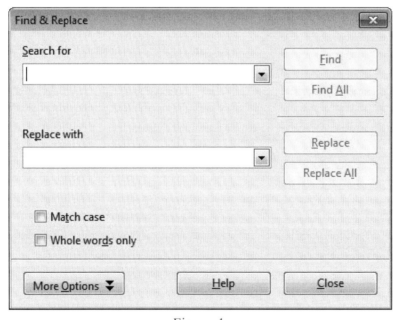

Figure 1

Note – The keyboard shortcut **CTRL + F** will also open the Find & Replace dialog box.

Step 4: In the **Search for** textbox, enter a word that is somewhere within the document and then click **Find**.

Step 5: Once Find has been clicked, the first occurrence of the word entered into the textbox will be highlighted within the document.

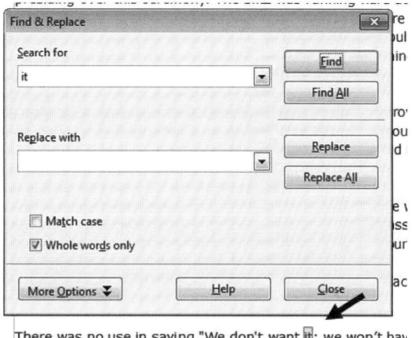

Figure 2

Note – Writer offers an option to search for only whole words. The **Whole words only** feature filters out other words that incorporate the desired word. For example, if the user is searching for the word "**swamp**" and they leave the **Whole words only** unchecked, other words such as "**swamped,**" will be selected. The Whole words only option is found in the **Find & Replace** dialog box.

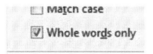

Figure 3

Writer also allows the user to search for every occurrence of particular word within a document. The following steps outline how this is done.

Step 1: Open the **Find & Replace** dialog box.

Step 2: Enter the desired word into the **Search for** textbox and click **Find All**.

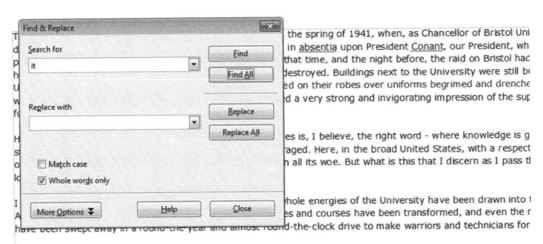

Figure 4

Step 3: Once **Find All** has been clicked, all occurrences of the word entered into the textbox will be highlighted within the document.

Replacing Text

Writer allows users to not only find text within a document, but also replace the text with another word. Writer provides two options when using this feature; the user can replace all occurrences of a particular word or phrase, or they can view each occurrence before deciding if replacing the text is necessary. The following steps explain how this is done.

Step 1: Open the **Find & Replace** dialog box.

Step 2: In the **Search for** textbox, enter the desired text.

Step 3: In the Replace portion of the dialog box, enter the preferred replacement text into the **Replace with** textbox.

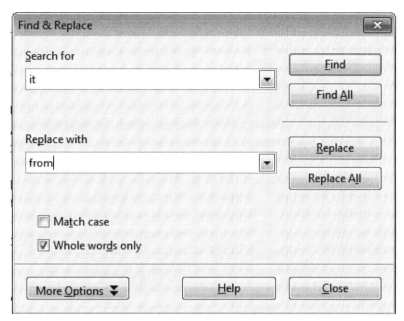

Figure 5

Step 4: To find the first occurrence of the text entered in **Step 2**, click **Find**. The first occurrence of the text will be highlighted within the document.

Step 5: Here, the user has the option of replacing the highlighted text with the preferred text entered in **Step 3**. To replace the text, click **Replace**. To leave the text in its current state, click **Find**.

Step 6: Repeat **Step 5** until all necessary text has been replaced.

Step 7: When Writer has shown the user every occurrence of the text entered in **Step 2**, a dialog box will appear with the message "OpenOffice Writer has searched to the end of the document. Do you want to continue at the beginning?" If the user would like to go back through the document, they can do so by clicking **Yes**. If not, they can click **No**.

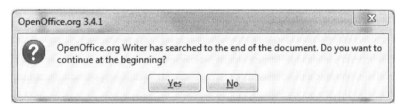

Figure 6

115

Writer also allows users to replace specified text throughout an entire document all at once. The following steps outline how this is done.

Step 1: Open the **Find & Replace** dialog box.

Step 2: In the **Search for** textbox, enter the desired text.

Step 3: In the Replace portion of the dialog box, enter the preferred replacement text into the **Replace with** textbox.

Step 4: Click **Replace All**. A dialog box will appear informing the user of how many replacements were made.

Figure 7

Step 5: Click **OK**, and then click **Close**.

Growth & Assessment

1. What tool in OpenOffice Writer allows users to find specific text within a document?

2. When replacing words in Writer, users are able to either replace them individually or all at once.

    a. TRUE

    b. FALSE

3. What does the Find All button do?

4. How would a user filter out other 'partial words' when searching for a desired word in Writer?

Section 2.10 – Using AutoCorrect

Section Objective:

- Learn how to use AutoCorrect.

Using AutoCorrect in Writer

OpenOffice Writer has a feature called AutoCorrect that is used to correct misspelled words within a document. The AutoCorrect feature will automatically correct a misspelled word as the user types. It can also suggest corrections for grammatical errors, such as incomplete sentences, misuse of a word, and misplaced punctuation. Though this feature is a helpful tool, the user may want to disable certain types of automatic corrections and this can be done by changing the AutoCorrect options. The following steps will outline how to disable a common type of automatic correction (capitalizing the first letter of every sentence).

Step 1: Open a previously saved Writer document.

Step 2: Click **Tools**, located on the Menu Bar.

Step 3: Within the Tools drop-down menu, select **AutoCorrect Options....** The AutoCorrect dialog box will appear.

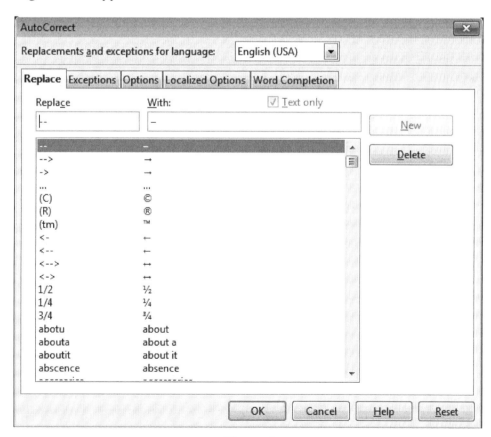

Figure 1

Step 4: Click the **Options** tab.

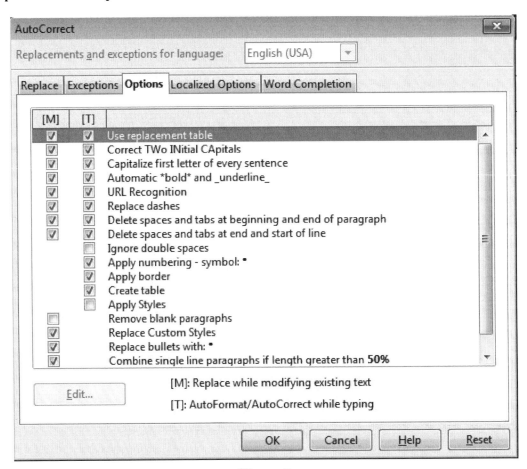

Figure 2

Step 5: **Uncheck** the **Capitalize first letter of every sentence** checkbox.

Step 6: Click **OK**. AutoCorrect will no longer automatically capitalize the first letter of every sentence.

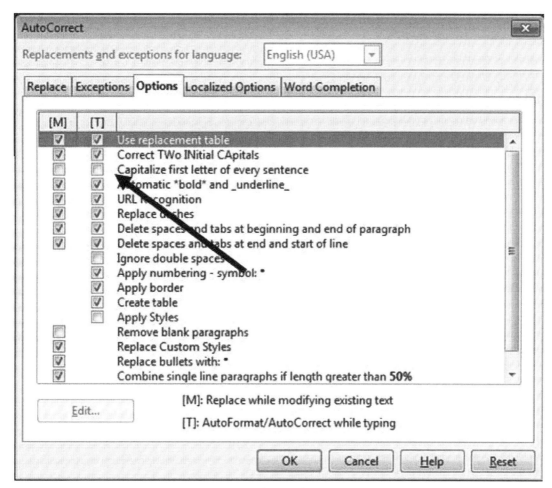

Figure 3

Adding New Words to the AutoCorrect Library

New words can be added to the **AutoCorrect library** and will thereafter be recognized by the AutoCorrect feature. The following steps outline how this is done.

Step 1: Create a new Writer document and type the word "**comppposition**." Since the word is not recognized by Writer, it will have a wavy red line under it.

> **Note** – This exercise is designed to teach the user how to add a word to the Auto-Correct library. The word "**comppposition**" is not a real word.

Figure 4

Step 2: Click **Tools**, located on the Menu Bar.

Step 3: From the Tools drop-down menu, select **AutoCorrect Options…**. The AutoCorrect dialog box will appear.

Step 4: Click the **Replace** tab.

Step 5: In the **Replace** window add "**comppposition**" into the **Replace** textbox and "**composition**" in the **With** textbox.

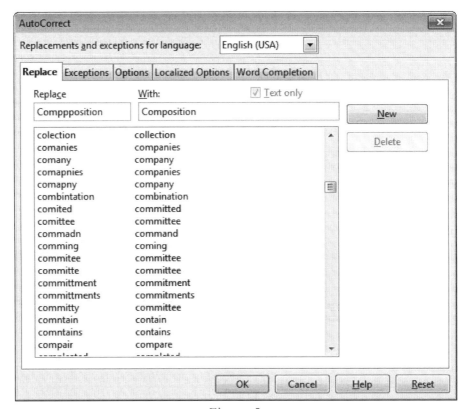

Figure 5

Step 6: Click **OK**. Writer will now recognize "**comppposition**" and automatically replace it with "**composition**."

Growth & Assessment

1. What is the feature in Writer that automatically corrects misspelled words?

2. What else can AutoCorrect fix?

3. Users can turn off the feature that automatically capitalizes the first letter of a new sentence.

    a. TRUE

    b. FALSE

4. What can users do if AutoCorrect does not recognize a word?

Section 2.11 – Creating a Table

Section Objective:

- Learn how to create and present data in a table.

Using Tables in Writer

OpenOffice Writer allows users to insert tables into a document. Writer provides the user with two options for inserting tables into a document. The first option is to use a preformatted table and the second option is to use the Drag method. The **Drag** method offers a more customizable approach to inserting a table. Both options are outlined below.

Table Terminology

Before covering how to insert a table into a Writer document, three key terms must be introduced.

- **Column** – A column is the vertical portion of a table. Columns run from top to bottom within a table.

- **Row** – A row is the horizontal portion of a table. Rows run from left to right within a table.

- **Cell** – A cell is a single unit within a table where a column and a row intersect. Data is inserted into the cells of a table.

Inserting a Preformatted Table

Step 1: Open a new Writer document.

Step 2: Click **Table**, located on the Menu Bar.

Step 3: From the Table drop-down menu, select **Insert** and then click **Table…**. The **Insert Table** dialog box will appear.

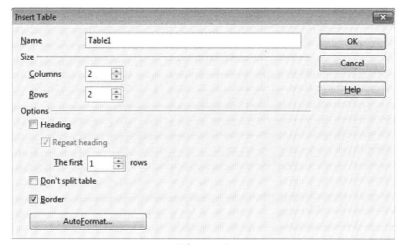

Figure 1

Step 3: In the **Name** portion of the dialog box, enter the preferred name for the table.

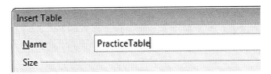

Figure 2

Step 4: In the **Size** portion of the dialog box, use the arrows to select the desired number of **Columns** and **Rows**.

Figure 3

Step 5: Click **AutoFormat**, located at the bottom of the dialog box.

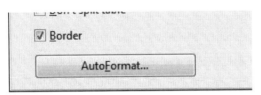

Figure 4

Step 6: Select the preformatted design, which will be applied to the table once inserted into the document.

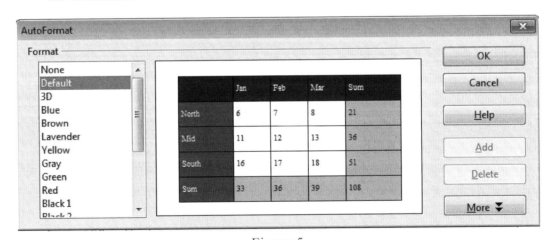

Figure 5

Step 7: Click **OK**. The AutoFormat window will close. Click **OK** again to close the Insert Table dialog box. A blank table will appear within the document.

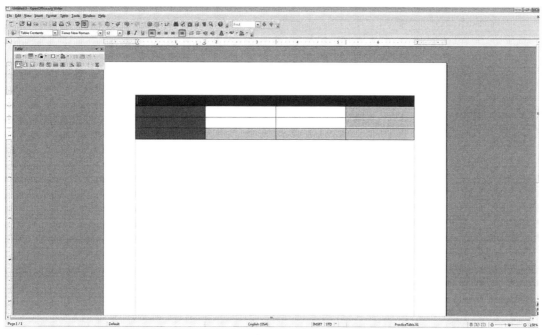

Figure 6

Note – The Insert Table dialog box can also be accessed by clicking the **Table** icon found on the Toolbar.

Figure 9

Inserting a Table Using the Drag Method

Step 1: Open a new Writer document.

Step 2: Click the arrow to the right of the **Table** icon on the Toolbar.

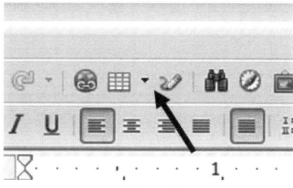

Figure 7

Step 3: A grid will appear. Position the cursor over the grid. The blue cells indicate the number of columns and rows that will be added to the table. A numerical value is also provided below the cells.

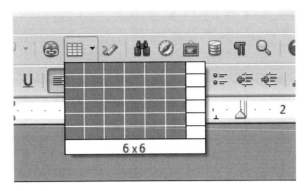

Figure 8

Step 4: Once the preferred table size has been chosen, click the bottom right blue cell. A table will appear within the document.

Growth & Assessment

1. What are the two main ways of inserting a table into a Writer document?

2. What is a column? What is a row?

3. Where is data inserted in a table?

4. Steve is using the Drag method to insert a table in Writer. He has selected 3 rows and 4 columns. How many cells will his table have?

Section 2.12 – Using AutoText

Section Objective:

- Learn to store and then reproduce a table using AutoText.

Using AutoText in Writer

OpenOffice Writer allows the user to easily store text formats, images and tables for quick access using the AutoText feature. The conventional method of copying and pasting bits of text, or manually inserting images within a document, can waste time and are inefficient. AutoText allows the user the permanently store these items within Writer for easier access. The following steps outline how to set up and use the AutoText feature of Writer.

Creating AutoText

Step 1: Open a new Writer document. Create a 3x3 table. Title the table as shown in the illustration.

Item	Price	Number Sold

Figure 1

Step 2: Hold down the left mouse button. Drag the cursor across the entire table until the entire table is highlighted.

Item	Price	Number Sold

Figure 2

Step 3: Click **Edit**, located on the Menu Bar.

Step 4: From the Edit drop-down menu, select **AutoText**. The **AutoText** dialog box will appear.

> **Note** – The keyboard shortcut **CTRL + F3** will also open the AutoText dialog box.

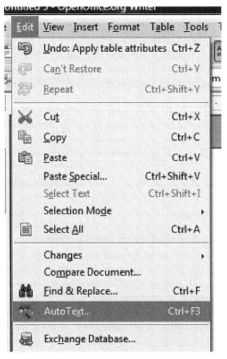

Figure 3

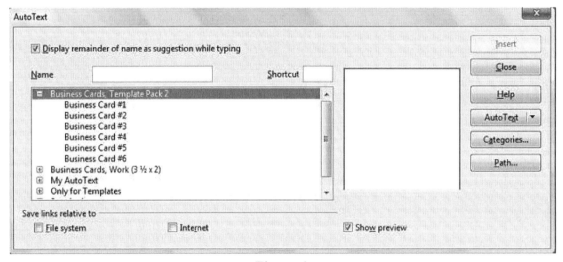

Figure 4

Step 5: With **My AutoText** selected, enter the preferred table name into the **Name** textbox.

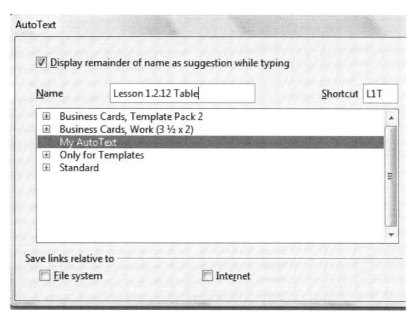

Figure 5

Step 6: If desired, type a shortcut into the **Shortcut** textbox. The shortcut can be used to reference the AutoText table later in the document.

   Note – Writer will suggest using "**L1T**" as the shortcut for the table.

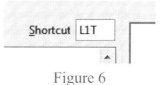

Figure 6

Step 7: Along the right side of the dialog box, click the **arrow** on the AutoText button and then select **New**.

Figure 7

Step 8: Click the **checkbox** next to **Show Preview** at the bottom of the dialog box.

Figure 8

Step 9: Click **Close**. The user will now be able to recreate the table as AutoText at any time.

127

Inserting AutoText

Step 1: Open a new Writer document.

Step 2: Press **CTRL + F3**. The AutoText dialog box will appear.

Step 3: Select the table name used when creating the AutoText.

Step 4: Click **Insert**. The table will be inserted into the document.

Growth & Assessment

1. AutoTable is a feature in Writer that allows users to store text formats, images and tables for quick access.

    a. TRUE

    b. FALSE

2. What is the keyboard shortcut to bring up the AutoText dialog box?

3. AutoText only temporarily stores information.

    a. TRUE

    b. FALSE

Inserting AutoText

Section 2.13 – Formatting Tables

Section Objective:

- Learn how to format tables.

Formatting a Table

OpenOffice Writer has many table formatting options to choose from. Two of the options are **Merge** and **Split**. Merge is used in Writer to merge multiple cells together to create one cell. Split is used to split a single cell into smaller cells. When using the splitting option, only one cell can be split at a time. The steps to use Merge and Split are outlined below.

Merging Cells

Note – Before merging cells in Writer, a table needs to be inserted into the document. Follow the steps below which explain how to use the *drag method* when inserting a table.

Step 1: Open a new Writer document.

Step 2: Click the arrow to the right of the **Table** icon on the Toolbar.

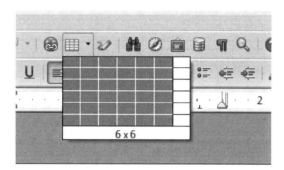

Figure 1

Step 3: A grid will appear. Position the cursor over the grid. The blue cells indicate the number of columns and rows that will be added to the table. A numerical value is also provided below the cells.

Figure 2

Step 4: Once the preferred table size has been chosen (for this example create a table that is at least 3x3), click the bottom right blue cell. A table will appear within the document.

Monday	Tuesday	Wednesday	Thursday	Friday	Saturday	Sunday

Figure 3

Now that a table has been inserted into the document, the user can merge the cells.

Step 5: Highlight the top row of the inserted cell.

Monday	Tuesday	Wednesday	Thursday	Friday	Saturday	Sunday

Figure 4

Step 6: **Right-click** anywhere within the highlighted row and select **Merge**.

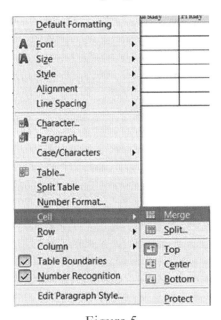

Figure 5

Step 7: Once Merge has been selected, the top highlighted row will become one single cell.

Monday Tuesday Wednesday Thursday Friday Saturday Sunday						

Figure 6

The Table Dialog Box

A quicker way to access **Merge** is to use the **Table** dialog box that opens when a new table is created. To access Merge, highlight the desired cells and click on the **Merge** icon in the **Table** dialog box. Once clicked, the highlighted cells will merge into one single cell.

Figure 7

Splitting Cells

Note – For the steps below, use the same document and inserted table that was used earlier in this section.

Step 1: Highlight the previously merged row of cells.

Step 2: Using the **Table** dialog box, click the **Split** icon. The **Split** dialog box will appear.

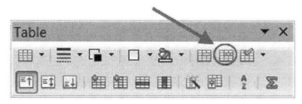

Figure 8

Step 3: In the **Split** portion of the dialog box, use the arrows next to **Split cell into** to select the preferred number of cells.

Step 4: In the **Direction** portion of the dialog box, select **Horizontally** or **Vertically**. Once the preferred direction has been identified, click **OK**. This will split the single merged cell back into individual cells.

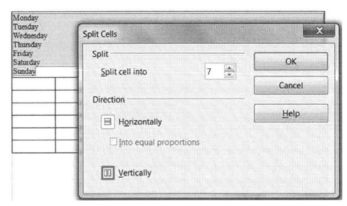

Figure 9

Moving a Table

Writer allows users to move a table within the text of a document. A table can be moved several ways; however, for the example below, the *drag method* will be used. The following steps outline how this is done.

Step 1: Position the cursor on the upper left-hand corner of the table until the Diagonal Arrow appears.

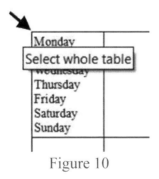

Figure 10

Step 2: Click the left mouse button once to highlight the table.

Step 3: Click and hold the left mouse button. Drag the highlighted table to the new position. Once the table is in the new position, release the mouse button and the table will be placed in the document.

Growth & Assessment

1. Two cells can be split at the same time.

    a. TRUE

    b. FALSE

2. What does Merge allow users to do?

3. Where can the Merge and Split icons be found?

Section 2.14 – Working with Table Data

Section Objective:

- Learn how to work with table data.

Working with Data

OpenOffice Writer has many formatting features that can be used when working with data within a table. One important aspect is the direction and flow of the text within a cell. Aside from the simple formatting changes such as, changing the font and size of the text, Writer allows the user to change the position of the text. Another important feature available in Writer is the ability to incorporate basic formulas into a table. The steps below outline how to change the position of the text within a cell, as well as how to use basic mathematical formulas within a table.

Changing the Text Position

Step 1: Open a new Writer document and insert a blank table.

Step 2: Enter text into one of the cells within the table.

Step 3: Highlight the cell that text was entered into.

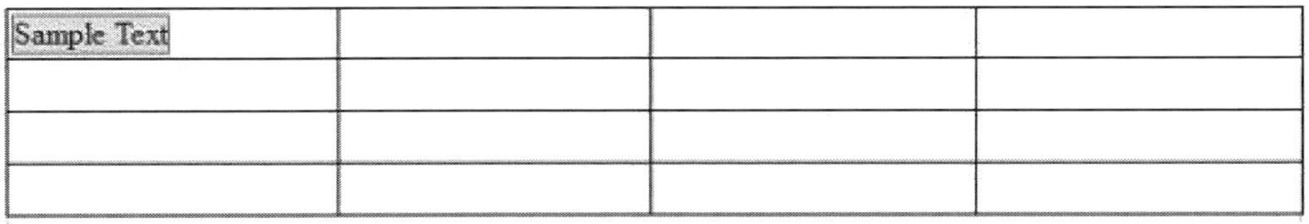

Figure 1

Step 4: Right-click the highlighted cell and select **Edit Paragraph Style…**. The **Paragraph Style: Table Contents** dialog box will appear.

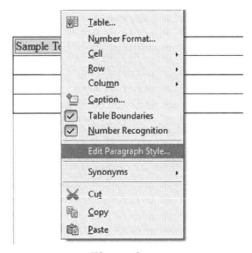

Figure 2

Step 5: Click on the **Position** tab located at the top of the window.

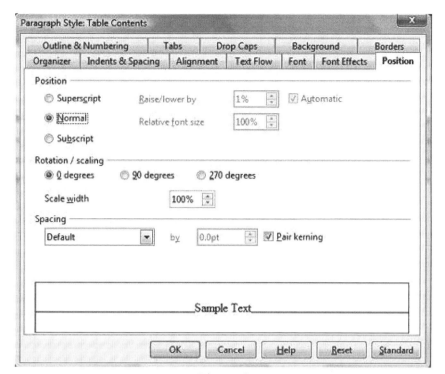

Figure 3

Step 6: In the **Rotation/scaling** portion of the dialog box, click the radio button next to the desired degree.

Note – Selecting **90 Degrees** will make the text vertical with the top of the text facing left. Selecting **270 Degrees** will make the text vertical with the top of the text facing right.

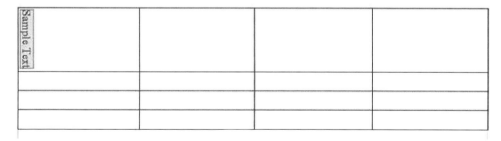

Figure 4

Step 5: Once the desired degree has been selected, click **OK**.

Formulas

Addition, subtraction, multiplication and division are the four most basic mathematical formulas. The user has the ability to use these within a table. The steps to insert a formula are outlined below.

Note – Before covering formulas, the commonly used formula symbols need to be introduced.

> * - Shows multiplication
>
> ＋ - Shows addition
>
> - - Shows subtraction
>
> / - Shows division
>
> ( ) - Shows order of operations

Step 1: Place the cursor within a blank cell in the table.

Step 2: Click **Table**, located on the Menu Bar.

Step 3: From the Table drop-down menu, select **Formula**. The **Formula** bar will appear below the Menu Bar.

> **Note** – Pressing **F2** will also open the **Formula** bar.

Figure 5

Step 4: Enter "=(5*6)+45" into the **Formula** bar. Be sure NOT to use spaces between the characters.

Figure 6

Step 5: Once the characters have been typed into the Formula bar, press **Enter**. The answer to the formula will be inserted into the selected cell.

Figure 7

Growth & Assessment

1. Writer does not allow users to format the data within a table.

    a. TRUE

    b. FALSE

2. What are the three text position options?

3. What is the answer to "(3*2)-2"?

Section 2.15 – Using Columns to Present Text

Section Objective:

- Learn how to present text in columns.

Using Columns in Writer

The standard text layout of a text document in OpenOffice Writer is arranged as a single column; however, Writer offers many column options. Writer also allows the user to modify each column added to the document. The following steps outline how this is done.

Formatting Columns within a New Document

Step 1: Open a new Writer document. Place the cursor in the top left corner of the page.

Step 2: Click **Format**, located on the Menu Bar.

Step 3: From the Format drop-down menu, select **Columns…**. The Columns dialog box will appear.

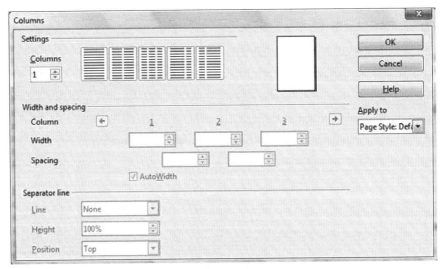

Figure 1

Step 4: Within the **Settings** portion of the Columns dialog box, use the arrows to select the preferred number of columns.

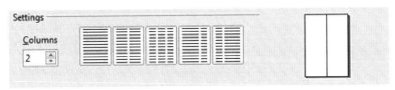

Figure 2

Step 5: Once finished click **OK**. The blank document will now have the number of columns selected in **Step 4.**

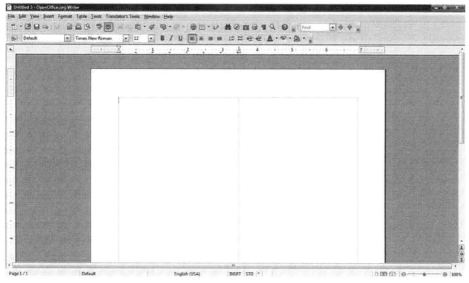

Figure 3

Formatting Columns within an Existing Document

Step 1: Open an existing Writer document and highlight a section of the text to format into columns.

Step 2: Click **Format**, located on the Menu Bar.

Step 3: From the Format drop-down menu, select **Columns…**. The Columns dialog box will appear.

Step 4: Within the **Settings** portion of the Columns dialog box, use the arrows to select the preferred number of columns.

Step 5: Once finished, click **OK**. The section of highlighted text will now have the number of columns specified in **Step 4**.

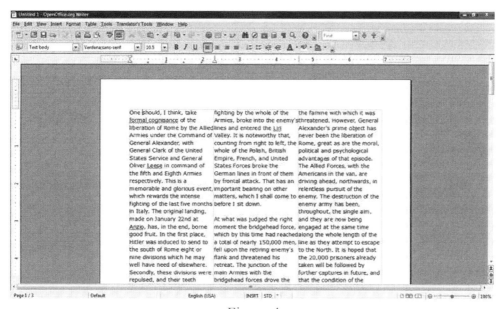

Figure 4

Formatting Column Width

Writer will automatically set the column width depending on how many columns are used. The default column width is 3.46 inches. Writer allows the user to reformat the column width, as well as the space between columns. The following steps outline how this is done.

Step 1: Use the steps above to insert three columns.

Step 2: Click **Format**, located on the Menu Bar.

Step 3: From the Format drop-down menu, select **Columns…**. The **Columns** dialog box will appear.

Step 4: Within the **Width and Spacing** portion of the dialog box, **uncheck** the **AutoWidth** checkbox.

> **Note** – When three columns have been inserted into a document, Writer, by default, sets the width of each column to 2.31 inches with 0 inches of space between them.

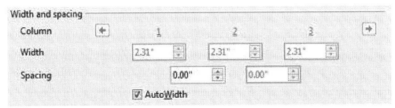

Figure 5

Step 5: Within the **Width and Spacing** portion of the dialog box, use the arrow keys to change the column width, and the width between the columns.

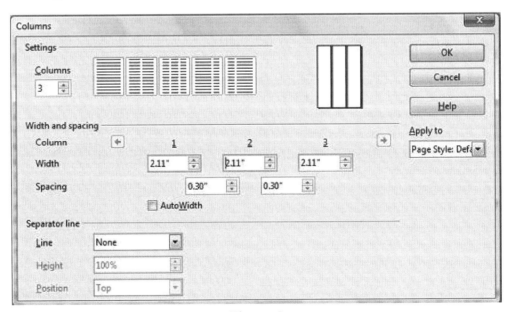

Figure 6

Step 6: Once the column width and the space between the columns has been selected, click **OK**. The changes will be applied to the document.

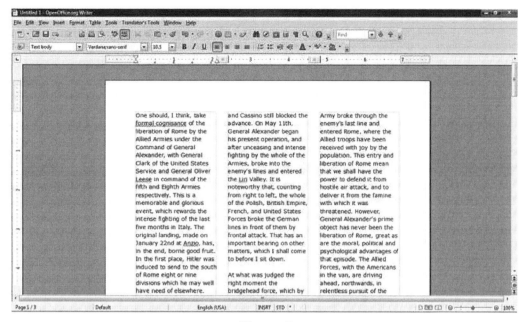

Figure 7

Growth & Assessment

1. What is the new column width, when three columns are inserted into a document?

2. What is the default column width?

3. What is the default space between columns?

Unit Three

Section 3.1 – Changing Font, Color, and Size   144

Section 3.2 – Using the Fontwork Gallery and ClipArt   149

Section 3.3 – Adding Headers and Footers to a Document   155

Section 3.4 – Adding Footnotes and Endnotes to a Document   159

Section 3.5 – Creating Custom Tab Stops   162

Section 3.6 – Indenting Text in a Document   165

Section 3.7 – Changing the Horizontal Alignment   169

Section 3.8 – Inserting a Manual Page Break   173

Section 3.9 – Adjusting Line Spacing in a Document   176

Section 3.10 – Using the Borders and Shading Tool   180

Section 3.11 – Using the Bullets and Numbering Tool   186

Section 3.12 – Sorting a List   188

Section 3.13 – Adding Symbols and Special Characters to a Document   191

Section 3.14 – Using Styles in a Document   194

Section 3.15 – Creating New Styles in Writer   199

Section 3.1 – Changing Font, Color, and Size

Section Objective:

- Learn how to change the font, color, and size of text.

Changing the Font, Size, and Color of Text in Writer

Writer allows users to change the font, size, and color of the text from the **Toolbar** and the **Character** dialog box, both located in the Writer Menu Bar. By providing all of these tools in one location, users can save time when making visual modifications to the text. This section will explain how to make these visual modifications, as well as cover how these formatting options can be changed by using the **Contextual Toolbar**.

Changing Text Using the Toolbar

The steps below outline how to change the font, size, and color of the text using the Toolbar, which is located on the Writer Menu Bar.

Step 1: Open a new Writer document and type one sentence. Then, select the text using the cursor.

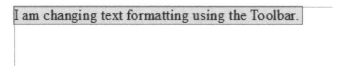

Figure 1

Step 2: In the **Formatting Toolbar**, located on the Menu Bar, click on the down-arrow next to the **Font** textbox. A drop-down menu with the Font options will appear.

Figure 2

Step 3: From the Font drop-down menu, select a font. Once a font has been selected, the text will change to the new font.

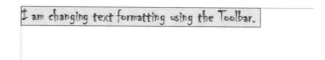

Figure 3

Step 4: With the text still selected, choose a different text size. This can be done from the **Font Size** drop-down menu.

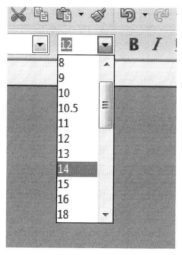

Figure 4

Step 5: At this point, both the font and size of the text has been changed. To select a new color, click the arrow next to **Font Color** and select from the various options.

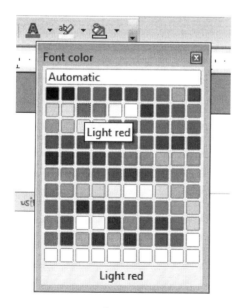

Figure 5

Changing Text Using the Character Dialog Box

A second way to change the font, size, and color of the text, also known as character formatting, is through the **Character** dialog box. The following steps outline how this task is done.

Step 1: Select the text.

Step 2: Select the **Format** menu located on the Menu Bar.

Step 3: Within the Format drop-down menu, click **Character....** The **Character** dialog box will appear.

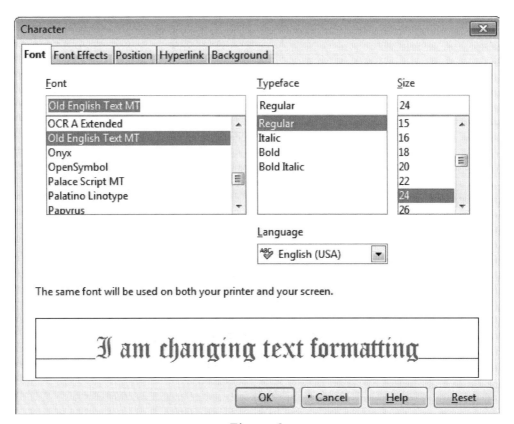

Figure 6

Step 4: Click on the **Font** tab at the top of the window.

Step 5: From the **Font** scroll list, select a font.

Step 6: From the **Size** scroll list, select a font size.

Step 7: Click on the **Font Effects** tab.

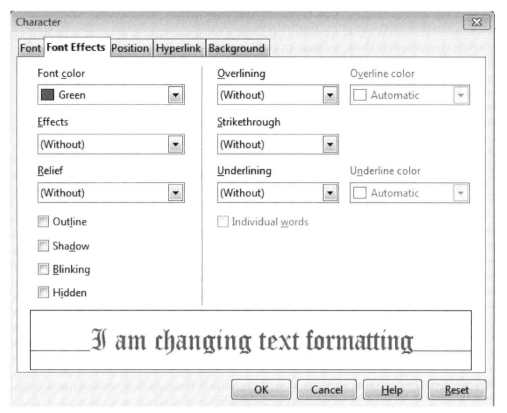

Figure 7

Step 8: In the **Font Color** drop-down menu, select a font color.

Step 9: Once the desired font, size, and color of the text has been selected, click **OK**.

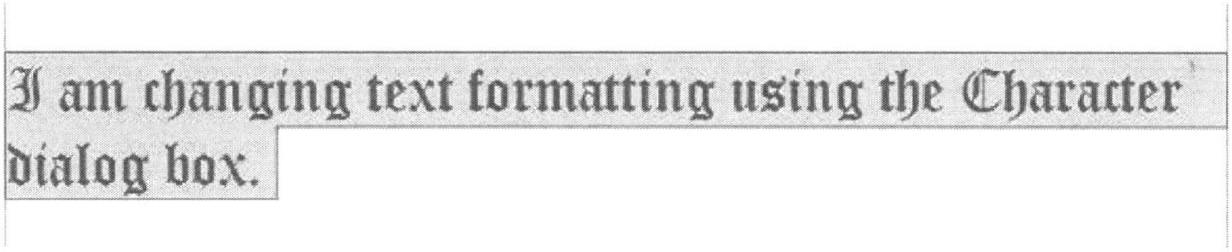

Figure 8

The Contextual Toolbar

Writer also allows users to change the font, size, and color of the text using the **Contextual Toolbar**. To open the Contextual Toolbar, right-click the highlighted text; the Contextual Toolbar will pop up. Within the Toolbar, make the desired text changes

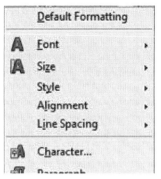

Figure 9

Growth & Assessment

1. Writer allows users to change the font, size, and color of text.

    a. TRUE

    b. FALSE

2. What two features found on the Menu Bar allow users to format text?

3. How would a user access the Contextual Toolbar?

Section 3.2 – Using the Fontwork Gallery and ClipArt

Section Objectives:

- Learn how to use the Fontwork Gallery.

- Learn how to insert ClipArt into a document.

The Fontwork Gallery

The Fontwork Gallery allows users to create graphic text art objects that can be used within Writer documents. This is a helpful feature when a user needs to add a creative touch or draw attention to something within a document. The Fontwork Gallery offers many options for text art objects such as positioning, size, area, and other various settings that allow users to create unique graphic objects.

The following steps outline how a user can create a text art object using Writer's Fontwork Gallery.

Step 1: Click on the **Fontwork Gallery** Icon from the **Drawing Toolbar** to access the Fontwork Gallery dialog box.

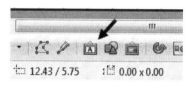

Figure 1

Figure 2

Note – If the Drawing toolbar isn't visible on the screen, go to **View > Toolbars > Drawing** to make it visible.

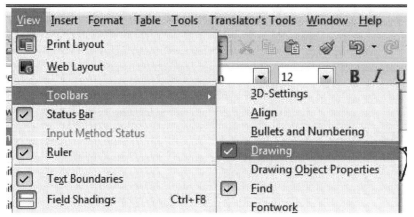

Figure 3

Step 2: Choose a design and click **OK**. The word "**Fontwork**" will be inserted into the document in the chosen design.

Figure 4

Step 3: Double-click anywhere within the inserted word art "(**Fontwork**)" to change the text.

Step 4: Resize the inserted Fontwork object. This is done by dragging the eight blue squares, referred to as *handles*, to adjust the size of the graphic object.

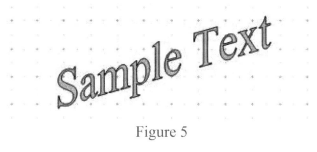

Figure 5

Step 5: Distort the inserted Fontwork object. Along with the eight blue squares, there is a yellow dot on the object. Position the cursor over the yellow dot and the cursor will change into a hand symbol. Once the cursor has made this transformation, the user can distort the Fontwork object by dragging the dot in different directions.

Figure 6

Step 6: Once the Fontwork object has been resized and distorted to the users preferred form, the object can be moved and positioned within the document. This can be done by positioning the cursor over the object until the cursor transforms into the dragging symbol. Once the dragging symbol is on the object, the Fontwork can be placed in the desired location within the document.

Inserting ClipArt

Writer allows the user to use a collection of free ClipArt by adding a free extension into the application. ClipArt are small digital pictures and pieces of art. By inserting ClipArt, a user can add visual appeal without having to design and produce a picture from scratch. The following steps outline how to incorporate ClipArt into a Writer document.

Step 1: Access the OpenOffice.org ClipArt extension page which can be found at the following link: *http://extensions.services.openoffice.org/en/project/oxygenoffice-gallery*

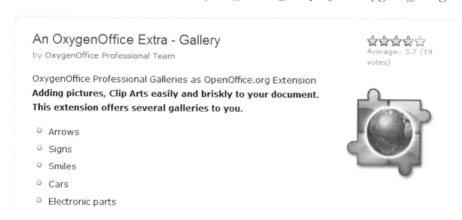

Figure 7

Step 2: Click **Get It!** to be directed to the **Download** page.

Figure 8

Step 3: Click on the manual download link to begin the download.

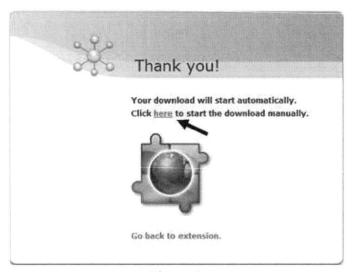

Figure 9

Step 4: When prompted, click **Open** on the File Download window.

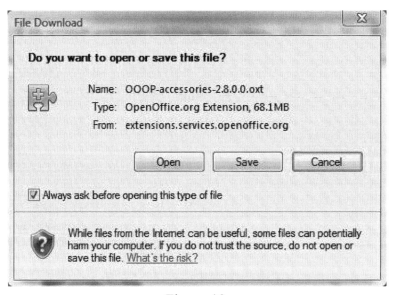

Figure 10

Step 5: Click **OK** and then click **Accept**, to accept the license agreement and begin installing **OOOP-Accessories**.

Figure 11

Step 6: The Extension Manager window will show that **OOOP-Accessories** has been added to Writer. Click **Close** and begin using the new graphics.

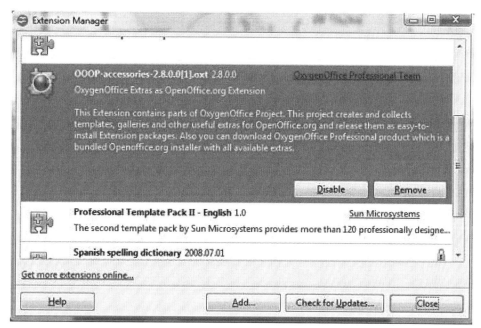

Figure 12

Once ClipArt has been added to Writer, the feature will allow users to insert new images by browsing through the **Gallery**. The following steps explain how to insert ClipArt.

Step 1: Create a new Writer document and select **Tools,** which is located on the Menu Bar.

Step 2: Within the **Tools** drop-down menu, click **Gallery**. This will cause the ClipArt task pane to appear at the top of the page window.

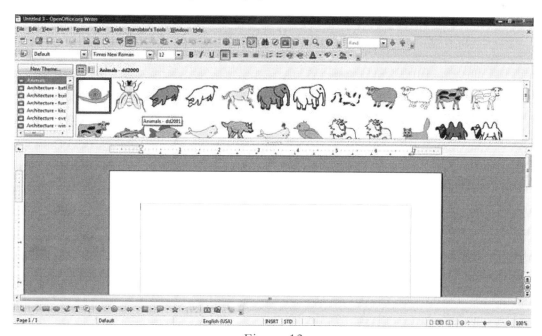

Figure 13

153

Step 3: Along the left-hand side of the task pane, there will be different folders displaying the different types of ClipArt available. Click on the desired type of ClipArt.

Figure 14

Step 4: Scroll through the selected ClipArt type and once an image has been selected, click on it and drag the image into the document.

Growth & Assessment

1. What feature in Writer allows the user to create graphical text art?

2. Font cannot be changed in the Fontwork Gallery.

    a. FALSE

    b. TRUE

3. What is ClipArt?

4. How would a user navigate to the menu bar which allows them to add the Drawing toolbar?

Section 3.3 – Adding Headers and Footers to a Document

Section Objective:

- Learn how to add headers and footers to a document.

Adding Headers and Footers to a Document

Headers and footers in OpenOffice Writer are located on the top margin (headers) and bottom margin (footers) of the document. The content within these areas is usually information such as, the name of the document, the page number, the date, and the author's name. The content is consistent throughout the document and is located in the same place (top and/or bottom margins) on every page.

Writer also allows the user to customize headers and footers to be page specific, meaning the user has the ability to change the headers and footers on a page by page basis. However, by default, identical headers and footers appear on every page of the document. This section will explain how a user can easily create headers and footers. The steps for this process are outline below.

Step 1: Create a new Writer document.

Step 2: Click **Insert** on the Menu Bar.

Step 3: Within the Insert drop-down menu, select **Header** and then **Default**. This will create a blank header within the document.

> **Note** – Follow the same steps when creating a blank **Footer**; however, choose Footer from the Insert menu instead of Header.

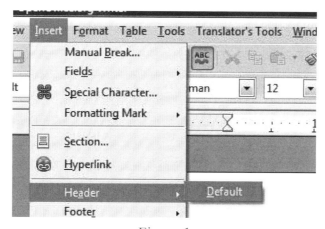

Figure 1

Figure 2

Here, Writer allows the user to manually type the desired text into the header/footer or select a preset field. The preset fields (complete list below) allow users to quickly add information to the header/footer without having to type everything in manually. The steps for inserting fields are outlined below.

Fields Available

- Date
- Time
- Page Number
- Page Count
- Subject
- Title
- Author

Inserting Fields

Step 1: Place the cursor within the blank header. On the **Ruler bar,** there will be 3 tabs set at different locations.

- Left Justified tab at 0 inches
- Center Justified tab at 3.5 inches
- Right Justified tab at 7 inches

Note – The curser defaults to the first tab, which is, *Left justified at the 0 inch mark*.

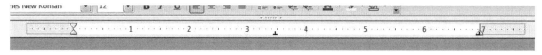

Figure 3

Step 2: Click **Insert** on the Menu Bar.

Step 3: From the Insert drop-down menu, click **Fields**. The list of available fields will open.

Figure 4

Step 4: Select the first field, **Date**. The current date will be inserted into the document.

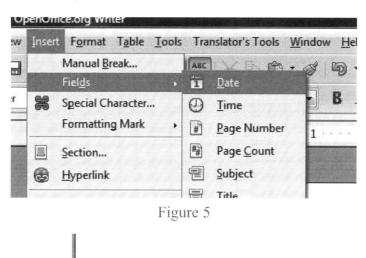
Figure 5

Figure 6

Step 5: Press the **Tab** button to move the cursor to the next tab on the Ruler bar. The cursor will be placed at, *Center Justified tab at 3.5 inches.*

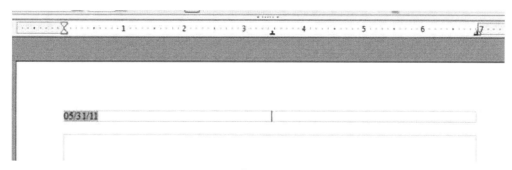
Figure 7

Step 6: Manually type in the desired text, or follow **Step 1** through **Step 4** to insert a new field.

Figure 8

Manually inserting text or inserting a field in the third position on the Ruler bar, which is *Right Justified tab at 7 inches*, can be done by repeating **Step 5** and **Step 6**.

Figure 9

Growth & Assessment

1. Where is the header located within a Writer document?

2. The footer is located along the left-hand margin of the document.

    a. TRUE

    b. FALSE

3. What are the three tab settings along the Ruler bar?

4. What are the optional fields in Writer?

Section 3.4 – Adding Footnotes and Endnotes to a Document

Section Objective:

- Learn how to add footnotes and endnotes to a document.

Adding Footnotes and Endnotes in Writer

OpenOffice Writer makes creating footnotes and endnotes effortless. Footnotes and Endnotes are used to provide extra information about the text. Footnotes are found at the end of the page that contains the referenced text and provide additional information about the referenced text and is also used by authors as a way to add comments about text. Endnotes are found at the end of a document and are most commonly used as citations for references which have been used in the creation of the document.

Writer automatically numbers the footnotes and endnotes created within a document. If a footnote or endnote is added, deleted, or moved, Writer will automatically renumber them accordingly. The following steps explain how to add footnotes and endnotes to a document.

Step 1: Open a previously saved Writer document and place the cursor where the footnote or endnote reference mark should be inserted.

Step 2: Click **Insert** on the Menu Bar.

Step 3: From the Insert drop-down menu, select **Footnote/Endnote…**. The **Insert Footnote/Endnote** dialog box will appear.

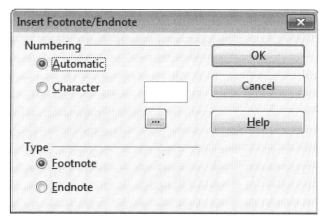

Figure 1

Step 4: By default, **Automatic** is selected as the numbering option. A user can choose a different character set by clicking on the ellipsis "**...**" button. The **Symbols** dialog box will open.

Note – If an Endnote is needed, click the **Endnote** radio button located under **Type** in the Footnote/Endnote dialog box. Writer will list the Endnotes at the end of the document.

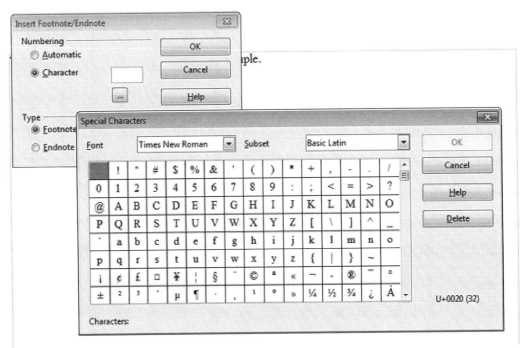

Figure 2

Step 5: After selecting a numbering set, click **Insert**. Once clicked, Writer will insert the note number "**1**" and will place the insertion point next to the note number.

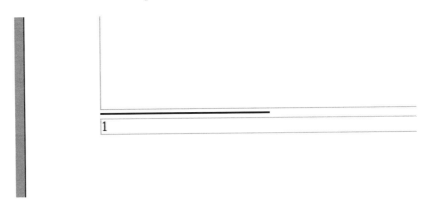

Figure 3

Step 6: Enter the note text.

Step 7: Double-click the note number to return to the reference mark that was previously created in **Step 1**.

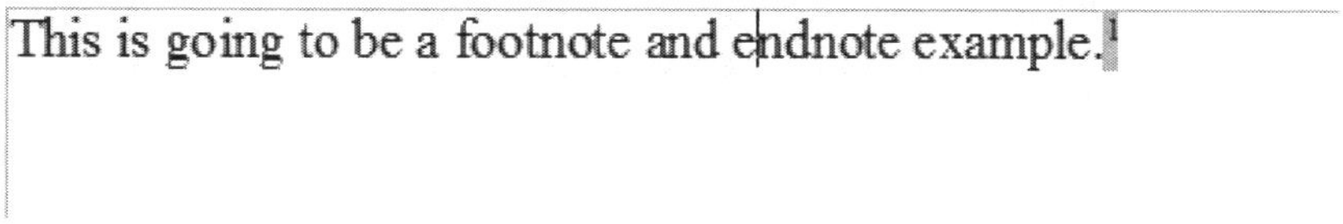

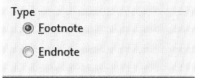

Figure 4

Figure 5

Growth & Assessment

1. Where are Footnotes found within a document?

2. Endnotes are found at the end of the page that contains the referenced text.

   a. TRUE

   b. FALSE

3. What button opens the Symbols dialog box?

Section 3.5 – Creating Custom Tab Stops

Section Objective:

- Learn how to create custom tab stops on the horizontal ruler.

Creating Custom Tab Stops

OpenOffice Writer allows the user to set and adjust tabs in a document using the Horizontal Ruler. The Horizontal Ruler allows the user to set, move, delete, or change tabs depending on the user's preference. If the Horizontal Ruler is not displayed, select **View**, located on the Menu Bar, and click the checkbox next to **Ruler**. Once the Ruler is displayed, the user can set custom tab stops. The following steps outline how this is done.

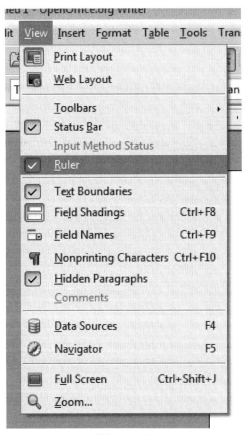

Figure 1

Step 1: Create a new Writer document or open a previously saved document.

Step 2: Select the portion of the document that will receive new tab settings.

Step 3: Click the **Tab Type** icon located in the top left-hand corner of the document until the **right justified** tab is selected.

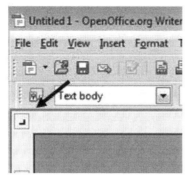

Figure 2

Step 4: On the horizontal ruler, click the preferred inch mark. This will cause a new right justified tab icon to appear on the ruler.

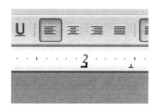

Figure 3

Once the new tab has been created, it can be adjusted by following the steps below.

Step 1: On the horizontal ruler, click and hold the tab that was previously created in **Step 4**.

Step 2: Drag the tab to a new inch mark and release the mouse button. This will cause the tab to move to the new location.

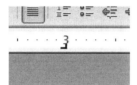

Figure 4

Writer allows users to quickly delete tabs that have been created. The steps below outline how this is done.

Step 1: Click and hold the previously created tab located on the horizontal ruler.

Step 2: Drag the tab into the document area of the screen and release the mouse button. This will cause the tab to no longer appear on the horizontal ruler.

Alternate Alignment Tabs

Writer offers four alignment tab options. They are shown below.

- Left
- Right
- Centered
- Decimal

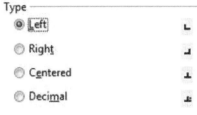

Figure 5

Growth & Assessment

1. Writer allows users to set and adjust tabs in a document using the horizontal ruler.

    a. TRUE

    b. FALSE

2. List the four alignment options in Writer.

3. The horizontal ruler is used as a guide for custom tab stops.

    a. TRUE

    b. FALSE

Section 3.6 – Indenting Text in a Document

Section Objective:

- Learn how to indent text in a document.

Indenting Text in a Document

Text indentation determines the distance of the text from either the left or the right margin. OpenOffice Writer allows the user to indent a single paragraph, a group of paragraphs, and create a hanging paragraph if that is preferred (a hanging paragraph is a paragraph in which the first line is not indented and the subsequent lines are). Though all three types of indentation mentioned are used, the most common type of indentation is the first line of a paragraph. The easiest way to indent the first line of a paragraph is to press the **Tab** button at the beginning of the paragraph. Writer also allows the user to indent manually. The steps to do this are outlined below.

Step 1: Open up an existing Writer document and click in front of the first line of the first paragraph.

Step 2: Click on the **Format** menu, which is located on the Menu Bar.

Step 3: From the Format drop-down menu click **Paragraph…**. The **Paragraph** dialog box will open with the **Indents & Spacing** tab selected.

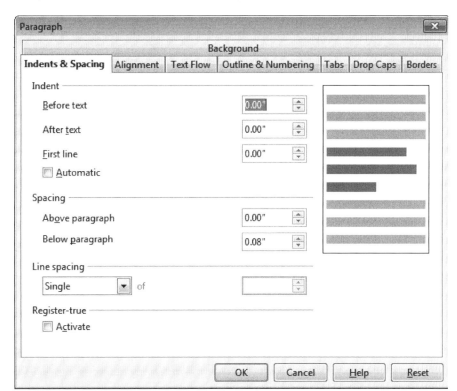

Figure 1

165

Step 4: Use the arrows next to **First line** to add the preferred indentation.

Figure 2

Step 5: Click **OK**. This will cause the first line of the paragraph to indent away from the left margin.

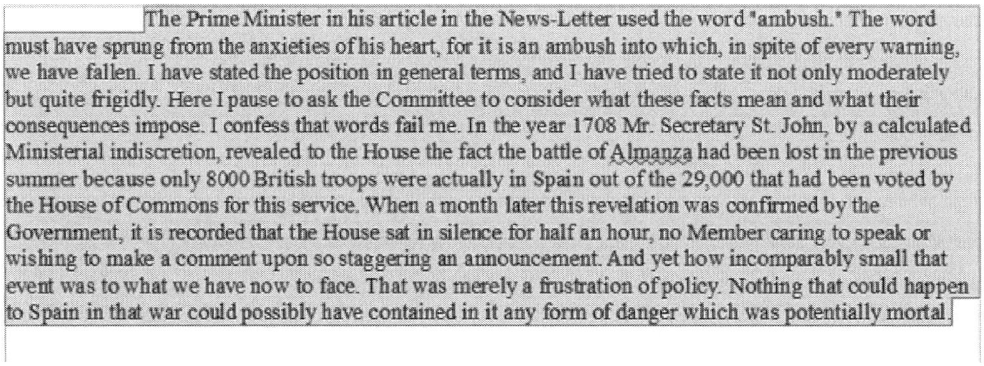

Figure 3

Indenting Entire Paragraphs

Writer also allows the user to indent an entire paragraph. This can be done by following the steps below.

Step 1: Highlight the first paragraph of the opened document.

Step 2: Click on the **Format** menu, which is located on the Menu Bar.

Step 3: From the Format drop-down menu click **Paragraph…**. The **Paragraph** dialog box will open with the **Indents & Spacing** tab selected.

Step 4: Use the arrows next to **Before text** to add the preferred indentation.

Figure 4

Step 5: Click **OK**. This will indent the entire paragraph to the specified amount.

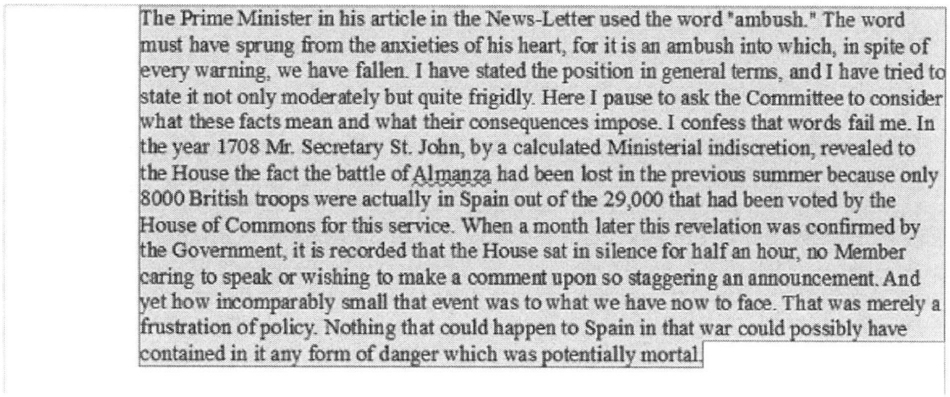

Figure 5

Note – If a number is entered in the **After Text** section of the window, the paragraph will indent from the right side of the page.

Hanging Paragraphs

As mentioned above, a hanging paragraph is a paragraph in which the first line is not indented and the subsequent lines are. This type of indentation is commonly used for lists and bulleted items. To create a hanging paragraph, follow the steps below.

Step 1: Open a recently saved document and use the left mouse button to select the first paragraph.

Step 2: Click **Format,** which is located on the Menu Bar.

Step 3: Within the Format drop-down menu, click **Paragraph…**. The **Paragraph** dialog box will open with the **Indents & Spacing** tab selected.

Step 4: Use the arrows next to **Before text** to add an indentation of **1.00″** (common indentation for a hanging paragraph).

Step 5: Use the arrows next to **First line** to change the indentation to **−1.00″**.

Figure 6

Step 6: Click **OK**. This will cause the paragraph to have a hanging indent of 1 inch.

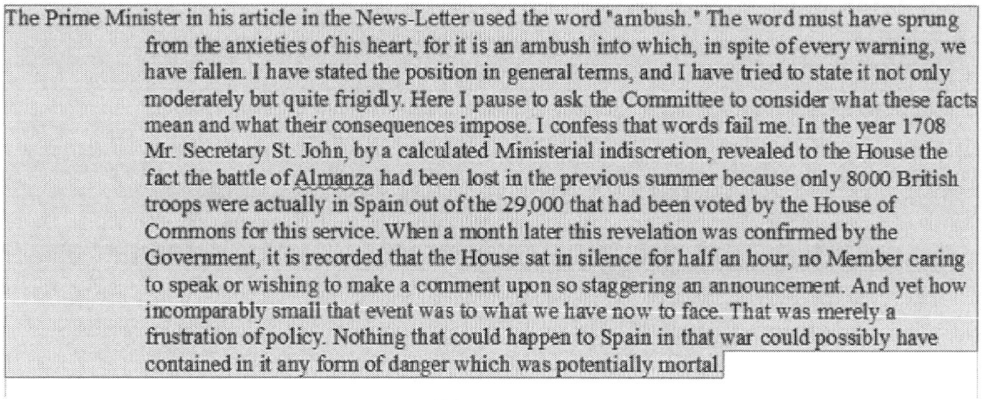

> The Prime Minister in his article in the News-Letter used the word "ambush." The word must have sprung from the anxieties of his heart, for it is an ambush into which, in spite of every warning, we have fallen. I have stated the position in general terms, and I have tried to state it not only moderately but quite frigidly. Here I pause to ask the Committee to consider what these facts mean and what their consequences impose. I confess that words fail me. In the year 1708 Mr. Secretary St. John, by a calculated Ministerial indiscretion, revealed to the House the fact the battle of Almanza had been lost in the previous summer because only 8000 British troops were actually in Spain out of the 29,000 that had been voted by the House of Commons for this service. When a month later this revelation was confirmed by the Government, it is recorded that the House sat in silence for half an hour, no Member caring to speak or wishing to make a comment upon so staggering an announcement. And yet how incomparably small that event was to what we have now to face. That was merely a frustration of policy. Nothing that could happen to Spain in that war could possibly have contained in it any form of danger which was potentially mortal.

Figure 7

Growth & Assessment

1. What is the most commonly used type of indention?

2. List two types of indention covered in this section.

3. Lists often use hanging paragraphs.

    a. TRUE

    b. FALSE

4. In which direction will the first line of a paragraph indent if the paragraph's First line is indented 2.50"?

Section 3.7 – Changing the Horizontal Alignment

Section Objective:

- Learn how to change the horizontal alignment of a paragraph.

Changing the Horizontal Alignment

OpenOffice Writer allows users to align text with the right or left margins, center the text, or align the text with both margins by adjusting the horizontal alignment. Changing the horizontal alignment will affect the entire paragraph; whether a single word is selected or the insertion point is placed within the paragraph, the entire paragraph will be altered. Adjusting the horizontal alignment of multiple paragraphs can be done as well. If this is desired, the user needs to identify which paragraphs they want to align. This can be done by selecting at least one character from each paragraph and then adjusting the horizontal alignment.

Using the Menu Bar

Before identifying which paragraphs to align, users must understand how the alignment can be changed. The following steps outline how changing the horizontal alignment can be done.

Step 1: Open a previously created Writer document and use the mouse button to select the entire text within the document.

Figure 1

Step 2: Click **Format** on the Menu Bar.

169

Step 3: From the Format drop-down menu, click on **Paragraph…**. The **Paragraph** dialog box will open.

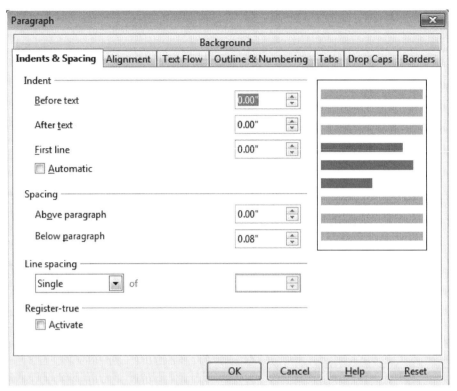

Figure 2

Step 4: Click the **Alignment** tab in the Paragraph dialog box to display the different alignment options available.

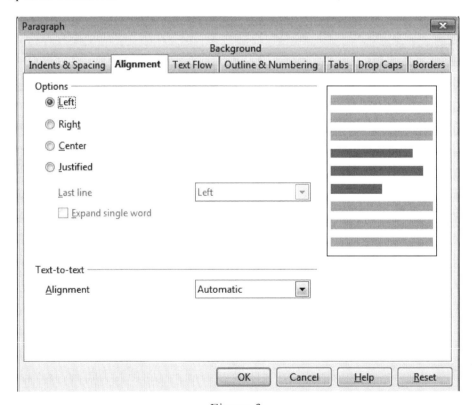

Figure 3

Step 5: Identify the type of alignment preferred by clicking the radio button next to the desired alignment, and then click **OK**.

> **Note** – A sample of the selected alignment will be displayed in the Paragraph dialog box. This is helpful when deciding which alignment is preferred.

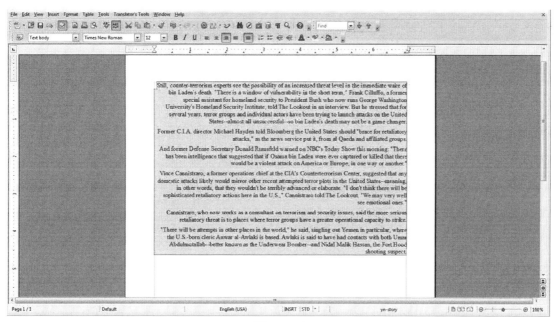

Figure 4

Using Alignment Buttons

Writer provides other tools that help users quickly adjust the alignment of the text without having to go through the Paragraph dialog box. The **Alignment Buttons**, located on the Toolbar, provide the same alignment options found in the Paragraph dialog box. These buttons however, allow the user to alter the alignment with a single click.

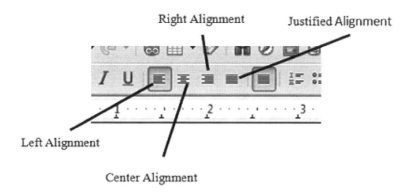

Figure 5

Using Keyboard Shortcuts

The third way to change the horizontal alignment in Writer is by using the keyboard shortcuts. By holding down the **CTRL + L** keys, a user can align the text with the left margin, and by holding down the **CTRL + R** keys, a user can align the text with the right margin. Writer provides these options to save the user time and effort when formatting a document.

Growth & Assessment

1. Changing horizontal alignment will affect the whole paragraph.

    a. TRUE

    b. FALSE

2. What is the keyboard shortcut to align the text with the left margin?

3. In which dialog box is the Alignment tab found?

Section 3.8 – Inserting a Manual Page Break

Section Objective:

- Learn how to insert a manual Page Break.

Inserting a Manual Page Break

OpenOffice Writer provides users with two types of page breaks. The first type is referred to as a natural page break. A natural page break occurs "naturally" as text is typed into a document and exceeds one page and moves to the next. The second type of page break is caused by manual force. This is often referred to as a **Manual Page Break**. Manual page breaks occur when the user manually inserts a hard page break. The following steps outline how this is done.

Step 1: Open a previously saved Writer document with multiple pages.

Step 2: Place the insertion point in the location where the page break is needed.

Step 3: Click **Insert**, which is located on the Menu Bar.

Step 4: From the Insert drop-down menu, select **Manual Break….**This will cause the **Insert Break** dialog box to appear.

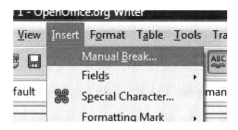

Figure 1

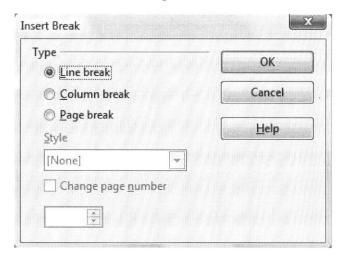

Figure 2

Step 5: If it is not already selected, click the radio button next to **Page Break**.

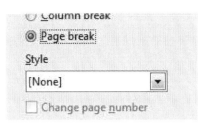

Figure 3

Step 6: Once the Page Break radio button is selected, select the preferred style. Writer provides the user with various page break styles and also allows the user to create their own style.

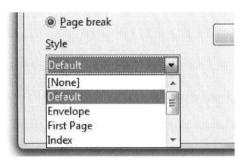

Figure 4

Step 7: If desired, click the checkbox next to **Change page number**. If checked, Writer allows the user to insert a new number for the first page after the page break.

Note – The Change Page Number option is helpful when working on research papers or other lengthy documents that require a cover page and table of contents because it allows the user to number the pages in a way that reflects the "true" first page of the paper.

Figure 5

Step 8: Once all of the selections required to set up the page break have been identified, click **OK**. This will cause the text after the insertion point to move to the next page.

Keyboard Shortcut

Writer also provides a keyboard shortcut for inserting a manual page break. By holding down **CTRL + ENTER**, a page break will automatically be inserted into the document and its location is dependent on the location of the insertion point. If a page break has never been inserted prior to using the keyboard shortcut, the style of the page break will be Writer's default style. If not, the style is based on previous use.

Note – An inserted page break can be deleted by selecting it with the mouse button and clicking **DELETE**.

Growth & Assessment

1. Writer offers how many types of page breaks?

2. What is a natural page break?

3. The keyboard shortcut to insert a manual page break is CTRL + SHIFT.

    a. TRUE

    b. FALSE

4. When would the Change Page Number option be used?

Section 3.9 – Adjusting Line Spacing in a Document

Section Objective:

- Learn how to adjust line spacing in a document.

Adjusting Line Spacing

OpenOffice Writer has a default line spacing of 1.0. This differs from other writing applications that tend to use a default line spacing of 1.15. Depending on the user's preference, Writer allows the default spacing of 1.0 to be changed. Changing the width of the space between the lines in a document can be beneficial for a number of reasons, some being: it can help the user better read the document, it provides space between the lines for note taking, and it can be helpful when editing a document by hand. The following steps explain how to adjust the line spacing to any needed width.

Step 1: Open a previously saved Writer document.

Step 2: Use the left mouse button to select the text.

Step 3: Click on the **Format** menu located on the Menu Bar.

Step 4: From the Format drop-down menu, select **Paragraph…**. The Paragraph dialog box will appear with the **Indents & Spacing** tab selected.

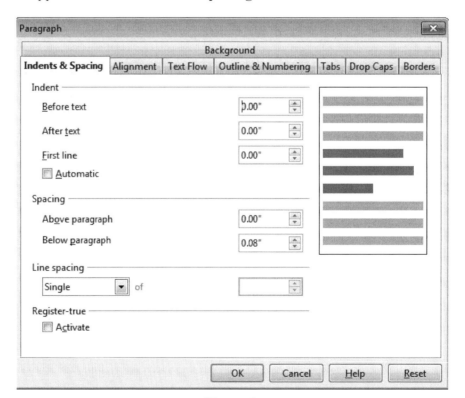

Figure 1

Step 5: In **Line spacing** portion of the dialog box, select the desired line spacing from the drop-down menu. The spacing options available in Writer are listed below.

Line Spacing Options

- Single
- 1.5 lines
- Double
- Proportional
- At least
- Leading
- Fixed

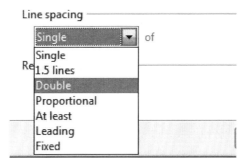

Figure 2

Step 6: After selecting the preferred spacing, click **OK**. The new spacing will be added to the selected text.

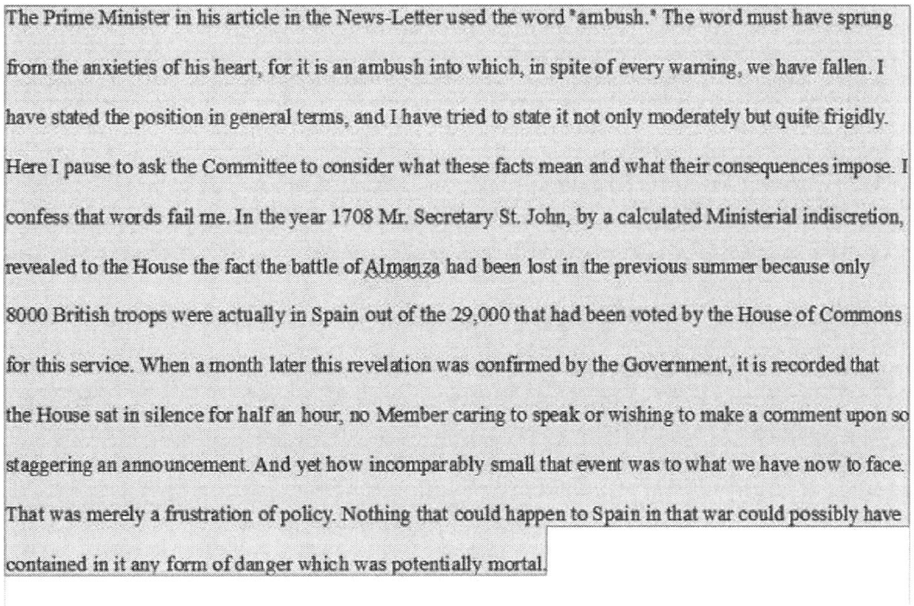

Figure 3

177

Writer also allows the user to adjust the amount of space before and after the paragraphs. The following steps outline how this done.

Step 1: Hold down the left mouse button and drag the cursor to select a paragraph.

Step 2: Click **Format** on the Menu Bar.

Step 3: From the Format drop-down menu, select **Paragraph…**. The Paragraph dialog box will appear with the **Indents & Spacing** tab selected.

Step 4: In the **Spacing** portion of the dialog box use the arrows to increase or decrease the spacing for both **Above paragraph** and **Below paragraph**.

Figure 4

Step 5: Click **OK**. This will cause the selected width to be inserted between the paragraphs.

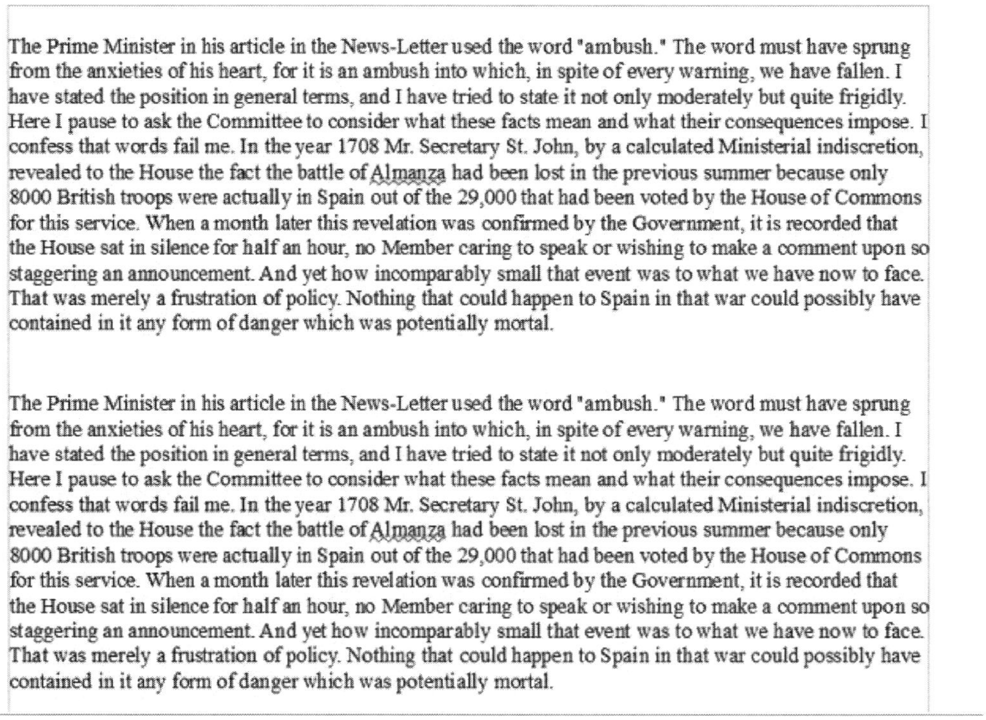

Figure 5

Note – The keyboard shortcut for 1.5 line spacing is **CTRL + 5**.

Growth & Assessment

1. List three line spacing options.

2. What is the default line spacing in Writer?

3. What is the keyboard shortcut for 1.5 line spacing?

4. Changing the spacing between lines is useful when editing a document by hand.

    a. TRUE

    b. FALSE

Section 3.10 – Using the Borders and Shading Tool

Section Objective:

- Learn about the Borders and Shading tool.

Boarders and Shading Tool

OpenOffice Writer, by default, applies a 0.05 point border and a white background with no shading to all tables and table cells created. The user however, has the option to add, remove, or modify table borders, and has the option to add shading to certain cells, rows, or columns in a table. The following steps explain how users can modify an inserted table by formatting boarders and using the shading tool.

Step 1: Open a new Writer document. Create a table using the Drag method and place the insertion point inside the table.

Step 2: Click **CTRL + A** to highlight the entire table, **Right-Click** anywhere in the table so that the **Quick Menu** appears.

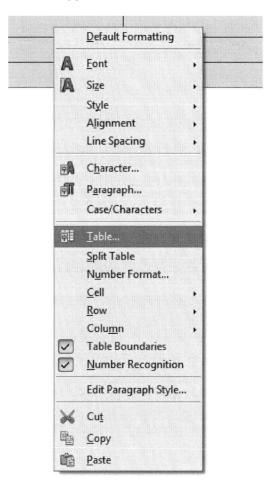

Figure 1

Step 3: From the Quick Menu, select **Table…**. The **Table Format** dialog box will appear.

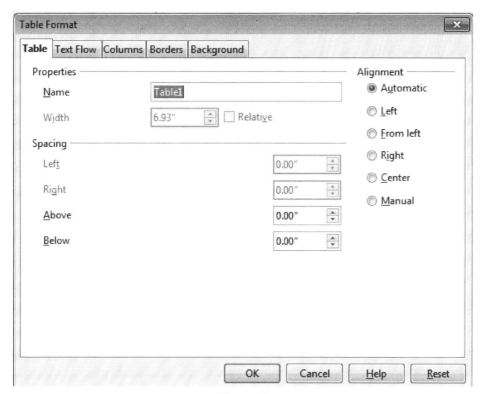

Figure 2

Step 4: Click the **Borders** tab at the top of the Table Format dialog box.

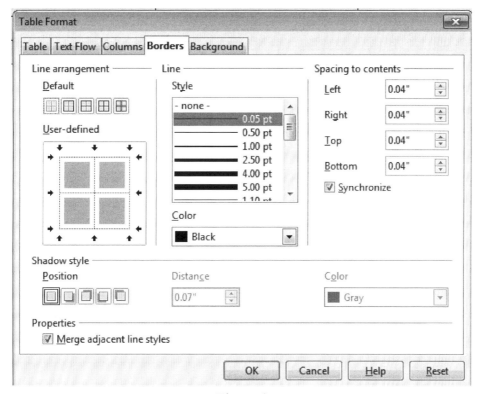

Figure 3

181

Step 5: The **Line arrangement** portion of the dialog box is where users have the ability to add boarders to the table. Writer provides the user with five preset options that offer different ways of applying boarders to the table. Select the preferred default line arrangement and make adjustments to the lines by customizing the lines in the **User-defined** area, which is located directly below the five line arrangement buttons.

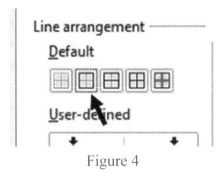

Figure 4

Five Preset Border Options

From left to right, they are:

- Set No Borders
- Set Outer Border Only
- Set Outer Border and Horizontal Lines
- Set Outer Border and All Inner Lines
- Set Outer Border Without Changing Inner Lines

Step 6: Determine the look of the border. The **Line** portion of the dialog box is where users have the ability to select the desired thickness of the boarder, as well as its color.

Figure 5

Step 7: The **Spacing to contents** portion of the dialog box is where users have the ability to select the desired width of the blank space between the border and the text. Adjust the spacing by clicking the arrows until each side's value is the preferred width. Writer also provides the **Synchronize** option that, when checked, applies the same spacing to all four sides of the table.

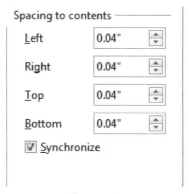

Figure 6

Step 8: Click **OK**. The selected border will be added to the table.

Figure 7

Shading Cells

As stated above, Writer provides the user with the option of shading the cells of the inserted table. The following steps explain how this is done.

Step 1: Place the cursor in any of the cells within the table.

Step 2: Right-Click in the cell that contains the cursor and click **Table…**. The **Table Format** dialog box will appear.

Step 3: Select the **Background** tab, which will display the shading options available in Writer.

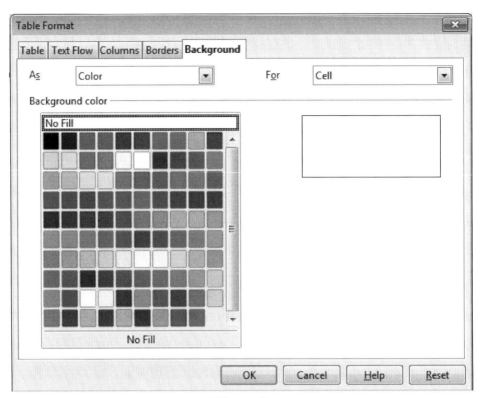

Figure 8

Step 4: Choose a preferred color from the available background shading options.

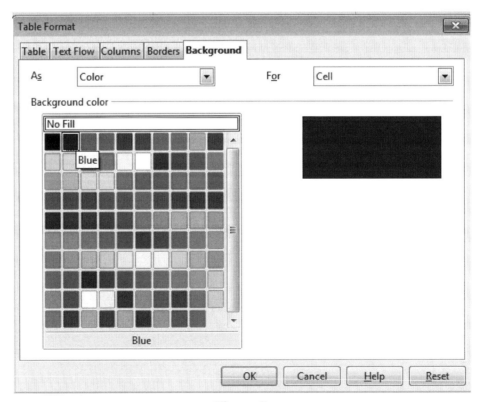

Figure 9

Step 5: Click on the arrow to expand the **For** drop-down menu. Select which section of the table will be shaded.

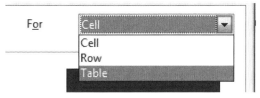

Figure 10

Step 6: Click **OK**. The selected shading will be added to the table.

Figure 11

Growth & Assessment

1. What is the default border size for all Writer tables and cells?

2. Users are able to add and remove table borders but not modify them.

    a. TRUE

    b. FALSE

3. How many preset border options does Writer offer?

4. List three preset border options.

Section 3.11 – Using the Bullets and Numbering Tool

Section Objective:

- Learn how to create and modify lists using the Bullets and Numbering tools.

Bullets and Numbering Tools

In OpenOffice Writer it is possible to create lists in a document by having Writer add bullet characters, or an automatically numbered list. There are two ways to have Writer add bullets or numbering to a document: they can be added by accessing the Toolbar and using the **Bullets or Numbering buttons**, or by going through the **Format** menu. This section explains how to add bullets and numbering to a document by using both of these options.

Steps for adding bullets to a list by using the Bullets button:

Step 1: Type a list of items to format.

Note – Press Enter at the end of each item so that each is contained in a separate paragraph.

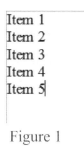

Figure 1

Step 2: Hold down the left mouse button and drag the cursor over the typed items to select them.

Step 3: Click the **Bullets** button, located in the Toolbar, to add bullets to the list.

Note – A numbered list can be created by clicking the **Numbering** button.

Figure 2

Writer will automatically rearrange the order of a numbered list if one or more of the items are deleted. Writer will also automatically update the list with a bullet or number if a new line is added by the user. The bullets and numbering can be removed from any item in the list by selecting the item with the cursor and clicking the button (Bullets or Numbering) a second time.

There are several added features in the **Bullet and Numbering Toolbar** that are available when creating a bulleted or numbered list. Users can create nested lists (where items in the list have sub-lists), change the style of a particular item listed, move items in the list and other options that are listed below.

Options available in the Bullet and Numbering Toolbar

- Bullets On/Off
- Numbering On/Off
- Move Up
- Move Down
- Move Subpoints Up
- Move Subpoints Down
- Restart Numbering
- Insert an Unnumbered Entry

Once a bulleted or numbered list has been created, Writer allows the user to change its format. The following steps explain how this is done.

Step 1: Hold down the left mouse button and drag the cursor over the list to select it.

Step 2: Use the formatting buttons on the Formatting Toolbar to change the various formatting options such as font, text size and color of the list. Once the preferred formatting options have been selected, they changes will be applied to the list.

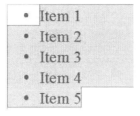

Figure 3

Growth & Assessment

1. What are two ways to have Writer add bullets or numbering to a document?

2. Users are able to change the text size of a bulleted or numbered list.

    a. TRUE

    b. FALSE

3. List four of the options available in the Bullets and Numbering Toolbar.

Section 3.12 – Sorting a List

Section Objective:

- Learn how to sort a list.

Sorting a List

OpenOffice Writer can automatically sort the items within a list. This is a helpful feature when a user has created a long list of items such as names, addresses and/or dates, and wishes to quickly sort them in alphabetical or numerical order. The following steps will outline how this is done.

Numerical Sorting

Step 1: Open a new Writer document and create a bulleted list.

- Bat
- Glove
- Ball
- Shoes
- Hat

Figure 1

Step 2: Drag the cursor over the entire list to select it.

Step 3: Click **Tools**, which is located on the Menu Bar.

Step 4: From the Tools drop-down menu, click **Sort…**. The **Sort** dialog box will open.

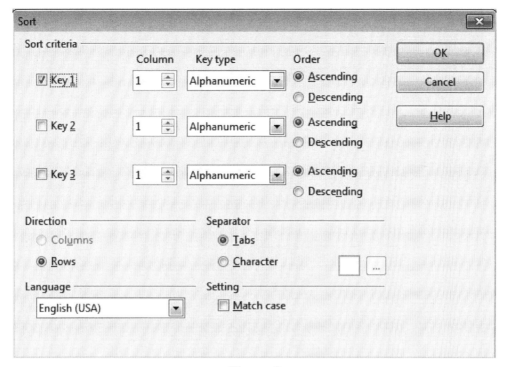

Figure 2

Step 5: Select the desired **Key type** in the **Sort criteria** portion of the dialog box. For example, if a user wanted to sort his classmates' age, he would select **Numeric** as the Key type.

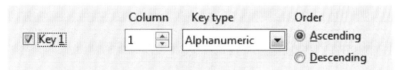

Figure 3

Step 6: Select how many columns are needed (the default is one column).

Note – For longer lists, users may want to add a second or third column to limit the number of pages within the document.

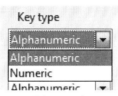

Figure 4

Step 7: Under **Order** there are two options available, **Ascending** or **Descending**. Both of these options are defined below.

Ascending – This option will sort the list from lowest to highest.

> Example: *1, 2, 3, 4, 5...*

Descending – This option will sort the list from highest to lowest.

> Example: *5, 4, 3, 2, 1...*

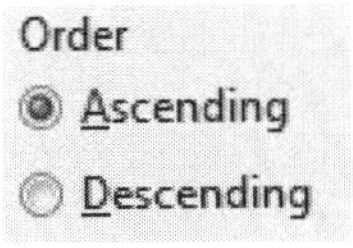

Figure 5

Step 8: Click **OK**. The list will be sorted using the guidelines specified in **Step 5** through **Step 7**.

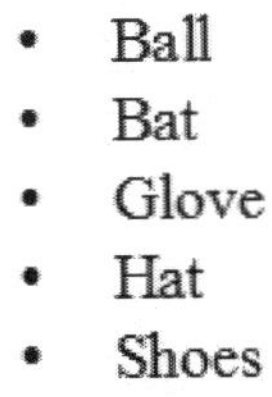

- Ball
- Bat
- Glove
- Hat
- Shoes

Figure 6

Alphabetical Sorting

The second order opting, **Alphabetical**, allows the user to order the items within the list alphabetically. This would be important if the user was making a roster of all of the players on a football team using their last names. Once a list is created, the user can apply the **Alphabetical** option in **Step 5** to better organize the list. Then the user can choose the order of the items; **Ascending** (a, b, c...) or **Descending** (z, y, x...).

Growth & Assessment

1. Writer can automatically sort the items within a list.

    a. TRUE

    b. FALSE

2. What are the two options used to order a list?

3. What type of order is used for a group of numbers, listed from highest to lowest?

4. How many sorting options are there?

Section 3.13 – Adding Symbols and Special Characters to a Document

Section Objective:

- Learn how to add symbols and special characters to a document.

Adding Symbols and Special Characters

OpenOffice Writer provides the user with various symbols and characters to use when working on a document. Many symbols and special characters are not available on the keyboard so they need to be accessed through the **Character** dialog box. The **Character** dialog box contains symbols, characters from other languages, arrows, and other special characters. All of these characters, once inserted into the document, can be formatted as if they were regular text. The following steps will explain how to insert symbols and other special characters.

Step 1: Open a new Writer document and place the insertion point where the symbol/character is needed.

Step 2: Click **Insert**, located on the Menu Bar.

Step 3: From the **Insert** drop-down menu, click **Special Characters…**. The **Special Characters** dialog box will appear.

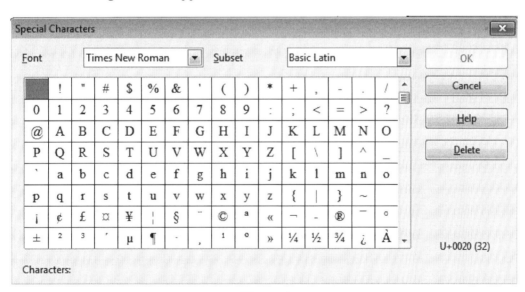

Figure 1

Step 4: Select the **Font** of the character or symbol that will be inserted into the document.

Figure 2

In the Special Character dialog box, the characters and symbols are broken down into subsets depending on their character type. For example, sigma ($\sum$) is a Greek letter, thus it would be under Basic Greek.

Step 5: Select the preferred character type from the **Subset** drop-down menu.

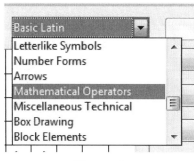

Figure 3

Step 6: The selected character type will appear in the Characters window. Click on the symbol or character that will be inserted into the documents and it will appear at the bottom of the window next to **Characters:**.

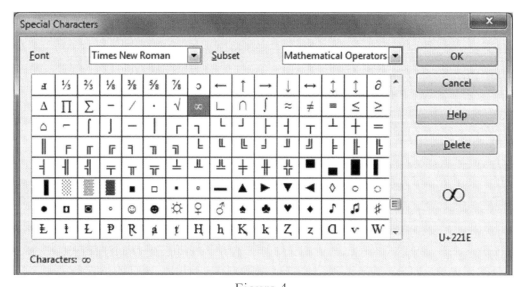

Figure 4

Step 7: Click **OK**. The symbol will then be inserted into the document.

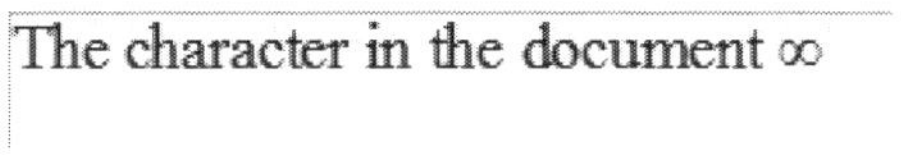

> The character in the document ∞

Figure 5

Note – Writer allows the user to insert multiple symbols at once. When the Character dialog box is open, click on multiple symbols before clicking the **OK** button. All of the selected symbols will be displayed next to **Characters:** at the bottom of the window.

Growth & Assessment

1. The Character dialog box contains characters from other languages.

    a. TRUE

    b. FALSE

2. What character type is the Greek letter phi (Φ)?

3. Writer allows users to insert multiple symbols at once.

    a. TRUE

    b. FALSE

Section 3.14 – Using Styles in a Document

Section Objective:

- Learn how to change the look of characters and paragraphs with styles.

Changing Character and Paragraph Styles

In OpenOffice Writer, changing styles are normally separated into two categories; change of character style, and change of paragraph style. Character styles format the font, font size, typeface, and color of the text. Paragraph styles format the same elements as character styles, but also modify the alignment, spacing, paragraphing, and indentation of the text. Writer provides the user with a selection of different styles to choose from and the following steps outline how this is done.

Step 1: Open a previously saved Writer document and use the cursor to drag and select the first paragraph of text. Once the text is selected, format the paragraph.

> **Note –** In order to change the paragraph style in a document that has been previously formatted, the user must format the paragraph and then create a style based on the most recent format. It is also important to understand that if the paragraph contains left and right indents, or a border, these formatting choices will also be part of the new style.

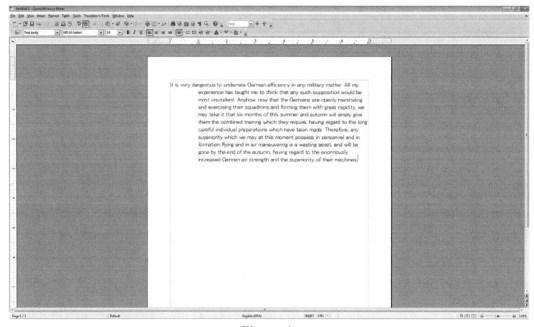

Figure 1

Step 2: Place the cursor within the newly formatted paragraph.

Step 3: Click **Format**, which is located on the Menu Bar.

Step 4: From the Format drop-down menu, select **Styles and Formatting**. The **Styles and Formatting** dialog box will open.

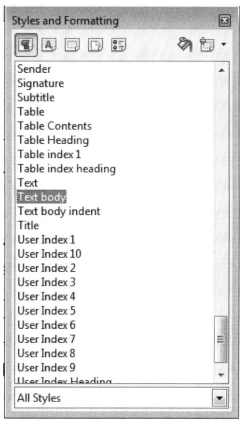

Figure 2

Note – Keyboard shortcut, **F11**, will also open the **Styles and Formatting** dialog box.

Step 5: Click the **Paragraph Styles** icon or the **Character Styles** icon, located at the top of the Styles and Formatting dialog box, and select which type of style is necessary.

Step 6: Click the **New Style from Selection** button, which is located in the top right-hand corner of the dialog box.

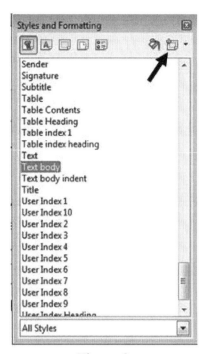

Figure 3

Step 7: From the options presented, **double-click** the preferred style and it will be applied to the selected text.

Figure 4

Modifying Existing Styles in Writer

When a new document is opened in Writer, it is based on the Default (blank page) template. Writer uses the Default style to determine the font, font size, line spacing, and parameters of the document. To modify Writer's default style, or any other available styles, follow the steps below.

Step 1: Click **Format**, located on the Menu Bar.

Step 2: From the Format drop-down menu, select **Styles and Formatting**. The **Styles and Formatting** dialog box will open.

Step 3: Click the **New Style from Selection** button, which is located in the top right-hand corner of the dialog box.

Step 4: **Right-click** the desired Writer style and select **Modify…**. The **Paragraph Style** dialog box will appear.

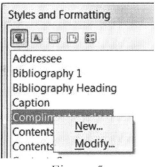

Figure 5

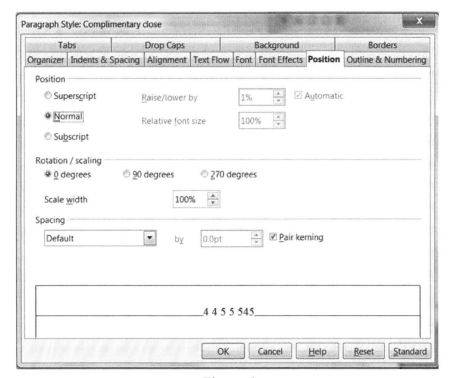

Figure 6

Step 5: Here, Writer allows the user to modify many aspects of the selected paragraph style. Once all modifications have been made, click **OK**. Now, the new modifications will be applied to the previously selected Writer style.

Growth & Assessment

1. Changing styles are normally separated into two categories.

    a. TRUE

    b. FALSE

2. What are the two styles?

3. Character styles format modify the alignment, spacing, paragraphing, and indentation of the text.

    a. TRUE

    b. FALSE

4. What is the keyboard shortcut for accessing the Styles and Formatting dialog box?

Section 3.15 – Creating New Styles in Writer

Section Objective:

- Learn how to create new styles.

Creating New Styles in Writer

OpenOffice Writer allows users to create custom styles to apply to the text. This feature allows users to name the new style, define the formatting characteristics, and select additional options which are covered below. Once a new style is created, Writer allows the user to apply it to the selected paragraph, or add it to the list of available styles. The following steps explain how to create a new, custom style.

Step 1: Create a new Writer document.

Step 2: Click **Format**, located on the Menu Bar.

Step 3: From the Format drop-down menu select **Styles and Formatting**. The **Styles and Formatting** dialog box will appear.

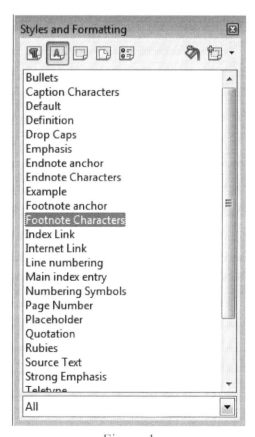

Figure 1

Note – Keyboard shortcut "**F11**" will also open the **Styles and Formatting** dialog box.

Step 4: Click the **Paragraph Styles** icon or the **Character Styles** icon, located at the top of the Styles and Formatting dialog box, to identify which type of style is necessary.

Step 5: Click the **New Style from Selection** button, which is located in the top right-hand corner of the dialog box.

Step 6: From the options presented, select **New Style from Selection**.

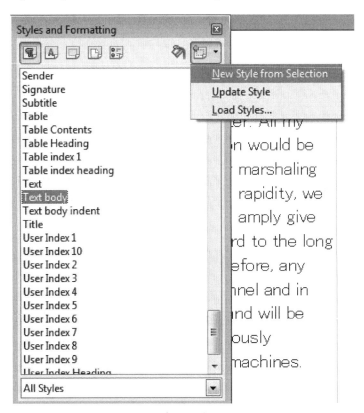

Figure 2

Step 7: The **Create Style** dialog box will appear. Here, Writer asks the user to name the new style. Enter in the new style name and then click **OK**.

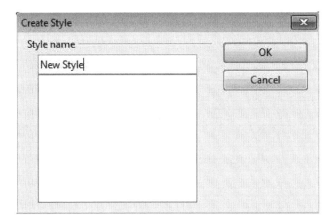

Figure 3

Note – The newly created, custom style will be added to the selection of available styles in the **Styles and Formatting** dialog box and can be used any time while working in Writer.

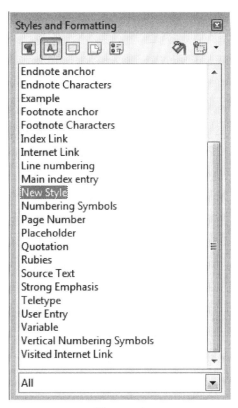

Figure 4

Step 8: Right-click on the style that was just created and select **Modify…**.

Up to this point, the two types of styles (**Paragraph Styles** and **Character Styles**) have required the same steps. At this point, Writer allows the user to modify various aspects of the new style. Depending on which style icon was selected in **Step 4**, the user will be presented with different style modification options. Below, the steps for making both types of modifications are outlined.

Modifying a New Character Style

Step 1: After right-clicking on the newly created style in **Step 8**, the **Character Style** dialog box will appear.

Step 2: Click the **Font** tab located at the top of the dialog box. Here, Writer allows the user to change the font, size, and typeface of the text for the new style. Once these have been selected, click **OK**.

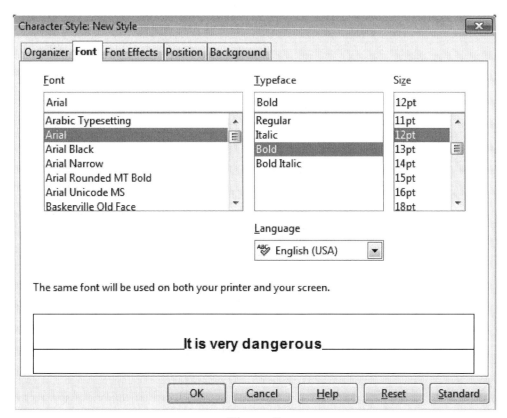

Figure 5

Step 3: Click the **Font Effects** tab, located to the right of the Font tab, to view the available **Color** options. Once a color has been selected, click **OK**.

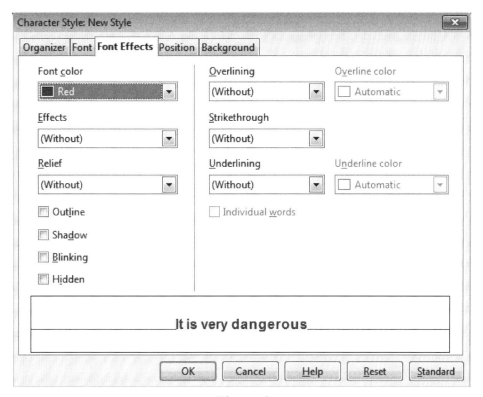

Figure 6

Step 4: Click on the newly created character style and close the **Style and Formatting** dialog box. This will apply the new style to the opened document.

Modifying a New Paragraph Style

Step 1: After right-clicking on the newly created style in **Step 8**, the **Paragraph Style** dialog box will appear.

Step 2: Click the **Indents & Spacing** tab located at the top of the window. In the Indents & Spacing portion of the dialog box, Writer allows the user to change the spacing, paragraphing, and indentation of the text for the new style. Once these have been selected, click **OK**.

Step 3: Click the **Alignment** tab, located next to the Indents & Spacing tab, to modify the alignment of the new style. Once the alignment has been identified, click **OK**.

Step 4: Click on the newly created paragraph style and close the **Style and Formatting** dialog box. This will apply the new style to the opened document.

> **Note** – Writer allows the user to delete a custom style by right-clicking on the style name in the **Styles and Formatting** dialog box, and selecting **Delete**. If a deleted style was being used by the document, Writer applies the original style to all paragraphs formatted with the deleted style.

Growth & Assessment

1. Writer allows users to create a custom style to apply to the text.

    a. TRUE

    b. FALSE

2. Character styles and Paragraph styles have the same modification options.

    a. TRUE

    b. FALSE

3. Where is the newly created, custom style added?

Appendix

OpenOffice Volume I: Writer Unit 1

Section 1.1

1. On the Menu Bar
2. Within the Table menu
3. Shortcut icons

Section 1.2

1. The Tips feature
2. By opening the Help menu and selecting What's This?
3. a. TRUE
4. Click the Find tab at the top of the Help Dialog Box, and in the Search text box, type saving a document

Section 1.3

1. a. TRUE
2. Select the Blank Document option
3. Any two of the following: letters, memos, resumes, forms

Section 1.4

1. Two
2. a. TRUE
3. A file name

Section 1.5

1. Either the user can close the document, keeping Writer open, or close the document and exit the application completely.

2. b. FALSE

3. The Close button is found under File in the Menu Bar.

Section 1.6

1. Answers will vary. Possible answer: The user can access the Print option in the File Menu.

2. b. FALSE

3. Any two: which pages to print, the order in which pages print, the number of copies

4. To use the shortcut when printing, press and hold CTRL and then press P.

Section 1.7

1. b. FALSE

2. .odt

3. .ott

4. .doc

Section 1.8

1. a. TRUE

2. While in Writer, select File and Open. Then choose the desired file to open.

3. Double-click the icon or right-click and select Open

Section 1.9

1. Margins can be changed in Writer by either using the Page Rulers or using the Format button located in the Menu bar.

2. Over the line between the gray and white sections of the page ruler

3. Portrait and Landscape

4. a. TRUE

Section 1.10

1. Print Layout View, Web Layout View, Full Screen Reading View

2. b. FALSE

3. a. TRUE

Section 1.11

1. The Navigator feature

2. b. FALSE

3. Zoom allows the user to adjust the size of the document.

Section 1.12

1. b. FALSE

2. The Format tab

3. Three: Addressee, Sender, Size

4. Sender

Section 1.13

1. b. FALSE

2. Any three of the five: Use the current document, Create a new document, Start from existing document, Start from a template, Start from a recently saved starting document

3. Letter and E-mail message

4. Make any necessary changes

Section 1.14

1. Three

2. a. TRUE

3. It allows the user to view the recently created salutations in the documents

4. b. FALSE

Section 1.15

1. a. TRUE

2. Preview and Edit Document

3. It allows the user to find a particular document

4. Four

OpenOffice Volume I: Writer Unit 2

Section 2.1

1. The clipboard stores temporary information while within a document.
2. b. FALSE
3. CTRL+ X
4. CTRL+ C

Section 2.2

1. b. FALSE
2. Quick Menu and through the Spelling and Grammar dialog box
3. Ignore All
4. b. FALSE

Section 2.3

1. Within the Header or the Footer
2. At the bottom of the documents, below the text
3. a. TRUE
4. Roman (i ii iii)

Section 2.4

1. b. FALSE
2. A time stamp is a feature of Writer that allows the user to show the time of the last edit or change to a particular section of a document.
3. Letters and memos

Section 2.5

1. Overplus; superfluity; embarrassment

2. Select Tools from the Menu bar. Select Language. Select Thesaurus.

3. b. FALSE

4. Word Count keeps track of the number of words and characters used in a document.

Section 2.6

1. Translator's Tool

2. a. TRUE

3. Translate Text

Section 2.7

1. A hyperlink is a connection between a particular section of a document, such as, a section within the text or a photo, and another location.

2. A hyperlink can be either: a between two or more sections within a document or a link between a section of the text and an outside source, such as a website.

3. a. TRUE

4. Highlight the hyperlink within the text. Right-click the highlighted hyperlink. Select Remove Hyperlink.

Section 2.8

1. Outlines help to organize ideas and thoughts that go into a piece of writing.

2. Within the Bullets and Numbering tool

3. To Promote a line means to shift it to the left. Demote means to shift a line to the right.

Section 2.9

1. The Find & Replace tool
2. a. TRUE
3. It finds all of the occurrences of the desired word
4. Check the Whole words only checkbox

Section 2.10

1. AutoCorrect
2. Grammatical errors
3. a. TRUE
4. Add that word to the AutoCorrect library and designate which word will replace it

Section 2.11

1. By inserting preformatted table or by using the Drag Method
2. A column is the vertical portion of a table. A row is the horizontal portion of a table.
3. Data is inserted into the cells of a table.
4. 12 cells

Section 2.12

1. b. FALSE
2. CTRL + F3
3. b. FALSE

Section 2.13

1. b. FALSE
2. Merge allows users to merge multiple cells into one cell.
3. Within the Table dialog box

Section 2.14

1. b. FALSE
2. 0 degrees, 90 degrees, 270 degrees
3. 4

Section 2.15

1. 2.31 inches
2. 3.64 inches
3. 0 inches

OpenOffice Volume I: Writer Unit 2

Section 3.1

1. a. TRUE
2. The Toolbar and Character dialog box
3. Highlight the text. Right-click using the mouse.

Section 3.2

1. Fontwork Gallery
2. b. FALSE
3. ClipArt are small digital pictures and pieces of art.
4. By first clicking View in the Menu bar. Then Toolbars. Then selecting Drawing.

Section 3.3

1. At the top of the document
2. b. FALSE
3. Left Justified tab at 0 inches, Center Justified tab at 3.5 inches, Right Justified tab at 7 inches
4. Date, Time, Page Number, Page Count, Subject, Title, Author

Section 3.4

1. At the end of the page that contains the referenced text.
2. b. FALSE
3. The ellipses "…" button

Section 3.5

1. a. TRUE
2. Left, Right, Centered, Decimal
3. a. TRUE

Section 3.6

1. First line
2. Any two of the three: first line, before text, or after text

3. a. TRUE

4. To the right

Section 3.7

1. a. TRUE

2. CTRL + L

3. Paragraph dialog box

Section 3.8

1. Two

2. A natural page break occurs "naturally" as text is typed into a document and exceeds one page and moves to the next.

3. b. FALSE

4. When writing a research papers or other lengthy documents that require a cover page and table of contents and the "true" first page actually begins, for instance, at page 7.

Section 3.9

1. Any three of the seven: Single, 1.5 lines, Double, Proportional, At least, Leading, Fixed

2. 1.0

3. CTRL + 5

4. a. TRUE

Section 3.10

1. 0.05 point
2. b. FALSE
3. 5
4. Any three of the five: Set No Borders, Set Outer Border Only, Set Outer Border and Horizontal Lines, Set Outer Border and All Inner Lines, Set Outer Border Without Changing Inner Lines

Section 3.11

1. Using the Bullets or Numbering buttons, or by going through the Format menu
2. a. TRUE
3. Any four of the eight: Bullets On/Off, Numbering On/Off, Move Up, Move Down, Move Subpoints Up, Move Subpoints Down, Reset Numbering, Insert an Unnumbered Entry

Section 3.12

1. a. TRUE
2. Ascending and Descending
3. Descending
4. Two

Section 3.13

1. a. TRUE
2. Basic Greek
3. a. TRUE

Section 3.14

1. a. TRUE
2. Paragraph and character
3. b. FALSE
4. F11

Section 3.15

1. a. TRUE
2. b. FALSE
3. To the Styles and Formatting dialog box

Made in the USA
San Bernardino, CA
17 January 2015